Holy
Week

Proclamation 4

Aids for Interpreting
the Lessons of the Church Year

Holy
Week

Gerard S. Sloyan

Series C

FORTRESS PRESS   PHILADELPHIA

Library of Congress Cataloging-in-Publication Data

Proclamation 4: aids for interpreting the lessons of the church year
  /Christopher R. Seitz.
    p. cm.
  Consists of 28 volumes in 3 series designated A, B, and C, which correspond to the cycles of the three year lectionary. Each series contains 8 basic volumes with the following titles:
Advent/Christmas, Epiphany, Lent, Holy Week, Easter, Pentecost 1, Pentecost 2, and Pentecost 3.
  ISBN 0-8006-4156-6
  1. Bible—Liturgical lessons, English. I. Seitz, Christopher R.
BS391.2.S37 1988
264'.34—dc19   88-10982

Printed in the United States of America   1-4156

95   94   93   92   91   2   3   4   5   6   7   8   9   10

Contents

Holy Week

The first use of the term "the church year" seems to have occurred in a *Postille* or sermon of a Lutheran pastor, Johannes Pomarius, in Wittenberg in 1589. So reports Adolf Adam in his extremely helpful *The Liturgical Year: Its History and Its Meaning after the Reform of the Liturgy.*[1] Easter is not the first recorded festal observance, as we might expect it to be. The Sunday is. Regular Sunday assembly by Christians is first hinted at when Saint Paul proposes the first day of the week as the day on which the Corinthian and Galatian communities should take up a collection for the famine-stricken Jerusalem Jews who believed in Jesus (1 Cor. 16:1–2). In Acts 20:7 Paul is further described as breaking bread on the evening of the first day of the week at Troas. The Book of Revelation also knows of a "Lord's day" on which its author was caught up in ecstasy (1:10). But since the fact of regular Sunday worship is not made absolutely clear in the New Testament there is the phenomenon (fairly recent, on a time line) of Christian Sabbatarianism as part of sixteenth- through nineteenth-century attempts to return to "primitive" practice.

Saint Ignatius of Antioch writes (ca. 110) that Christians live "in observance of the Lord's Day on which our life dawned through him and his death" (*To the Magnesians* 9.1–2). The *Didachē* or *Teaching of the Twelve Apostles* (ca. 80–130) has the precept, "On every Lord's Day—his special day—come together and break bread and give thanks, first confessing your sins so that your sacrifice may be pure."[2] The letter of Pliny to the emperor Trajan (ca. 165) reports that the Christians meet twice on Sunday, morning and evening, and Justin Martyr (ca. 155) tells how the service of Scripture readings, commentary, and the Lord's Supper was conducted. The latter was a ritual meal, presumably held early in the morning rather than a leisurely evening meal because of imperial decrees forbidding these, out of suspicion of evening gatherings.

A regularly recurring spring festival at Pesaḥ Time celebrating the death and resurrection of Jesus in a meal is first mentioned in the *Epistula Apostolorum* (130–40). Solid testimony to the observance of Easter comes late in the second century with mentions of it by

Apollonius of Hierapolis (ca. 170) and Melito of Sardis (before 190). Saint Paul had said in 1 Cor. 5:7–8 that since Christ "our paschal lamb" is sacrificed, the community with its old yeast removed should be a new dough. But while the annual observance of Passover was undoubtedly kept with a new intensity throughout the first century, there is no witness to Easter as a Christian feast in the New Testament or for more than a century following the resurrection. The "Quartodeciman controversy" of ca. 190 tells us most of what we know about it. The "fourteeners" (i.e., of the month of Nisan) of Asia Minor and Syria, Saint Polycarp of Smyrna among them, were holding to their custom of Easter on Pesaḥ according to the phases of the moon, on whatever day it fell. The Roman bishops Anicetus (d. 166) and Victor (d. 190) for their part maintained that the nearest Sunday was the sounder tradition. When the Sunday won out, it was the first full moon after the spring equinox in the West, but only if it falls after Passover in the East. The controversy is reported in full by Eusebius in his *History of the Church* (V.23–25) which he completed ca. 325. This was also the year of the Council of Nicea, which tried to put an end to the controversy. Eusebius tells of the rebuke administered to Bishop Victor by Irenaeus, bishop of Lugdunum (Lyon) in Gaul, for the excommunication procedure he attempted against the churches of the province of Asia. Eusebius does not give a source for who in fact sided with the East in the matter. Irenaeus wrote:

> The dispute is not only about the day, but also about the actual character of the fast. Some think that they ought to fast for one day, some for two, others for still more; some make their "day" last forty hours on end. Such variation in the observance did not originate in our own time, but very much earlier, in the time of our ancestors, who—apparently disregarding strict accuracy—in their naïve simplicity kept up a practice which they fixed for the time to come. In spite of that, they all lived at peace with one another and so do we: the divergency in the fast emphasizes the unity of our faith.[3]

The Nicean settlement meant that Easter could fall on any Sunday between March 22 and April 25 (when the fourteenth of Nisan fell on a Sunday, Easter was celebrated on the following Sunday), but never on the spring equinox itself, March 21. Meanwhile, the lunar calendar on which Easter was reckoned was losing out to a solar one in the Mediterranean world.

As late as 577 we find that the Spanish church had celebrated Easter on March 21, arrived at by its own erroneous calculation, while the Roman church observed it on April 18 and the churches using the Alexandrian system of nineteen-year lunar cycles (dating to 457) waited until April 25! Sometime around 525 an Eastern monk in Rome named Dionysius "the Little" translated into Latin the authoritative Easter tables which Cyril of Alexandria had drawn up some seventy-five years earlier. This eventually compelled a uniform observance among the Western churches, but not until the Venerable Bede in 731 popularized this system dating from the Incarnation (a refined chronology of that of Julius Africanus from about 225). Meantime, the Celtic system of an eighty-four-year cycle meant that practice in England and Ireland did not come into line with the other Western dating of Easter until the Synod of Whitby (664). Even today, the Orthodox East and some Catholic Eastern churches wait for the Sunday after the fourteenth of Nisan while the West does not, which means that the two observances can be as much as a lunar month apart.

The origin of the word "Easter" itself is disputed. The Venerable Bede thought that an Anglo-Saxon spring goddess Eostre was responsible for the name of the feast but there is little evidence that she had any such cult. The word "East" with reference to Christ's rising from the dead as the sun rises in the east may lie behind it (so wrote the twelfth-century Honorius of Autun). The Old High German *eostarun* for "dawn [*alba*]," a misconceived rendering of the "week in white vestments [*in albis*]," is another and perhaps the best explanation—similarly going back to the dawn which is the risen One.

More important to us than any of these chronologies or etymologies is the mid-fourth-century development which historicized the observance of the last days of Jesus' life. Up to that time a single feast of the crucifixion-resurrection had been celebrated on Sunday at dawn preceded by the customary night vigil of prayer. In the spring of 348 Cyril, a priest of Jerusalem, preached a series of catechetical lectures to mark the final instruction in the Creed and the Lord's Prayer of adult candidates for baptism. There he said nothing about the special observances described by Egeria (or Etheria), a pilgrim of means from Spain or Gaul in 383. From her we have a description of the Jerusalem observance in which she took part. Since the anonymous Pilgrim of Bordeaux (333), like Cyril himself, does not speak of the Easter liturgy, it is assumed that Cyril developed it during his long term as bishop (ca. 351–86)—an office from which he was thrice exiled by the Arians. Whatever the exact origin of the rites, it is from that period in Jerusalem that the Paschal observance became a matter of three days (Friday, Saturday, and Sunday) preceded by the Sunday of palm or olive branches.

Egeria tells how the Christians of Jerusalem gathered on the Saturday afternoon preceding Palm Sunday at the church on the site where Lazarus's sister Mary [*sic*] met Jesus (see John 11:29) and proceeded, singing psalms and antiphons, to the Lazarium, the site of his resuscitation. There a presbyter "proclaims about 'When Jesus came to Bethany' [John 11:55—12:11]" and "announces Easter." Egeria's account continues:

> The next day, Sunday, is the beginning of the Easter week or, as they call it here, "The Great Week." On this Sunday they do everything here as usual at the Anastasis ["Resurrection," a basilica on the site of the tomb probably built between 348 and 381] and the Cross [situated not far to the east] from cockcrow to daybreak, and then as usual assemble in the Great Church known as the Martyrium [the long nave built to the east of the court before the cross] because it is on Golgotha behind the Cross [a chapel in front of the south aisle of the Martyrium] where the Lord was put to death. (30.1)[4]

The service takes place in the Great Church "in the usual way" and then the archdeacon announces the week's activities, starting with reassembly, after a quick meal, at 1:00 P.M. in the Elaiona ["olive groves"] church on the Mount of Olives, an edifice erected by Constantine. Hymns and readings and prayers mark this early afternoon gathering. At 3:00 the bishop and people go to the Imbonon ["hillock"], the open "place" of the resurrection, for more of the same. At five o'clock the gospel is read about the children who met the Lord with palm branches, saying, "Blessed is he who comes in the name of the Lord" (Matt. 21:9, where "crowds" are spoken of; but see 21:15). Led by the bishop, all the people rise from their places and go down from the summit to the city and thence to the Anastasis, repeating "Blessed is he . . . ," singing psalms and antiphons all the while.

The best source we have for the psalms, antiphons, and readings used is the fifth-century Armenian Lectionary found in two manuscripts, one from Paris published at Oxford in 1905 and the other from Jerusalem cited in a catalogue published in 1948. For homilists interested in sharing the readings of Lent and the Paschal *triduum* ("three days") used in the city where the latter was first observed (plus readings of the major feasts from the Epiphany, January 6, to Saints Peter and Paul, December 28, and James and John, December

29), a convenient place to look is John Wilkinson's *Egeria's Travels*.[5] The work derives from the translation of Dom Athanase Renoux from the Armenian, in articles published between 1961 and 1965. The book contains extracts from six other authors, four of them from the fourth century, writing about the holy places.

Egeria says that in her part of the world they keep a fast of six weeks before Easter but in Jerusalem Lent (called *Heortae,* "Feasts," 27.1) lasts eight weeks. Neither Saturday nor Sunday is kept as a fast day in Jerusalem except for the Vigil of Easter, thus yielding forty-one weekdays of fasting. The daily divine offices do not seem to feature Scripture readings. These are confined to the eucharistic celebrations. "The sermons are frequent and lengthy, those of the presbyters preceding that of the bishop, "so that the people will constantly be learning about the Bible and the love of God" (25.1).[6] Egeria is edified by how well the bishop and his presbyters know the Bible, never failing to answer her quite intelligent queries about its contents. The bishop always recites the prayers, reads from the Scriptures, and preaches in Greek, although she assumes he knows Syriac. A presbyter at his side translates everything into Syriac during the liturgies while the Latin-speaking pilgrims like her get ready help from some of the "brothers and sisters" (here monks and nuns, although she was more used to the term as describing the baptized) who know Latin as well as Greek.

Saint Cyril's employment of Jerusalem's unique *genius loci* ("the spirit of the place") in his church's celebration of the Great Week has left its traces on all Christian celebration of the mystery of human redemption. The fact that the word "feast" could be used to describe a fast—all fasting was voluntary, Egeria writes, but some went from receiving the Eucharist on Palm Sunday until that of Easter without eating a morsel—or that Egeria can describe a reading largely of Jesus' passion as "the account of the Lord's resurrection" (24.10)[7] is indicative of the unity in her mind of the sufferings and exaltation of Christ as a single mystery. But it was Cyril's placing of the events of Jesus' last (and first!) days at the place and time where they occurred that influenced the Christian world to distinguish between the suffering or penitential aspects of their faith and the joyful ones.

"He alone of all the bishops of the world," Wilkinson writes, "could read of the events of the passion and resurrection in the very places mentioned in the Bible, and he made good use of his opportunities, as Egeria bears witness."[8] To Cyril's reforms the Christian world owes Palm Sunday with or without a procession, the Lord's Supper on Holy Thursday, the Veneration of the Cross on Good Friday, and the Easter Vigil—first restored experimentally in the West by the Roman Church in 1951. The Three Hours Devotion (which seems, in the fifth-century Armenian Lectionary of Jerusalem, to have actually lasted four) has no continuous history. The present practice, fairly widespread in some Protestant churches, was introduced in Peru by Jesuits after an earthquake of 1687. The lighting of the Holy Fire in the darkness of Saturday/Sunday does not seem to have been done in Egeria's day, but it surely developed from the daily *Lynchnicon* (Lat., *Lucernare*) between 4:00 P.M. and dusk, a lighting of lamps and candles in the Anastasis (Egeria 24.4).

The *modern* conclusion of the Lenten days begins with the "Palm Sunday of the Passion of Christ"—a uniting of the commemorations of the entrance of Jesus into Jerusalem and of his sufferings and death there—and ends on Wednesday. The fact that Cyril's historically commemorative celebration ultimately made its way to the West sometime around A.D. 450 should not distract modern Western congregations from fidelity to the shape of their earlier Paschal liturgies. At Rome in the time of Leo I (d. 461) the Last Supper, the passion and death, and the resurrection had not yet been separated and were still being observed as the one eschatological mystery. This was the case even though the passion was already being read on Palm Sunday and Leo was preaching seven of his nineteen homilies on it on that day. The Roman Holy Week of the sixth century seems to have consisted of a strict fast every day, an assembly without the Eucharist on Wednesday and Friday, and the Paschal vigil on Saturday night with its reception of new Christians in baptism and chrismation followed by the celebration of the Eucharist at midnight. The dramatic elements such as a Palm Sunday procession, the sung rendition of the passion gospels, the "reproaches" *(improperia)* and Good Friday Veneration of the Cross came from Syria by way of French and Spanish sources between the seventh and the fourteenth centuries. They were "only slowly and reluctantly accepted by the Papal rite," according to Anglican scholar Dom Gregory Dix.[9] They continued to prevail in the tide of medieval passion piety which flooded Catholic Europe. This emphasis in Christian prayer was, if anything, intensified by the Reformation.

A relic of the centrality of Jesus' passion is the present practice of reading the "long gospel" of Matthew, Mark, and Luke in successive years on Palm Sunday. In the lectionary of Trent it was Matthew on Sunday, Mark on Tuesday, and Luke on Wednesday. This seemingly Rome-initiated custom of giving Palm Sunday a passion character not only was not eliminated by the recent liturgical reforms that followed the Second Vatican Council but has been taken up by the many Protestant congregations which have lately adopted lectionary preaching. Because so few people relative to their numbers in all the communions observe Good Friday liturgically, the Palm Sunday practice assures their hearing the passion once a year. But the phenomenon is not unlike the modern custom—tragically concurred in by the churches—of celebrating Advent as a four-week feast of the Nativity. The chief difference is that the displacement of emphasis in spring is the matter of one day, not an entire month. An important pastoral consideration, as clergy and church musicians know, is that people are going to attend the churches in great numbers on Palm Sunday for whatever reasons. This scarcely seems a justification, however, for a week-long anticipated historical remembrance of the death of Jesus, which with his resurrection *is* the Easter mystery.

Because this matter of emphasis is so important, the commentary that follows is going to urge upon its readers a serious consideration of Luke 19:28–40 as the only fit gospel to be preached on, on Palm Sunday, rather than large portions of Luke 22 and (or) 23. The hymnic consideration of the upcoming memorial of the mystery of human redemption, Phil. 2:5–11, proposed by all the lectionaries, is pastorally very effective. In this spirit, a notable lack of enthusiasm will be expressed in these pages for reading from the Servant Songs of Isaiah 42, 49, 50, or 52—53 on Palm Sunday, for the reasons given above. The Lutheran proposal that Deut. 32:36–39 be read, which speaks of the God who is Lord of death and of life, is a solid one. It sets the tone for the Lent about to end as basically a time of fasting and religious study. This season will die on Thursday and the Paschal *triduum* will be celebrated from Friday to Sunday. To feature the commemoration of human redemption by reading two chapters of Luke one week before the feast occurs can be pastorally self-defeating. It is to invite Christians, however unconsciously, not to take Maundy Thursday or Good Friday seriously, and to view the resurrection as an anticlimax to the Lenten weeks that have erroneously been made to peak on Good Friday.

Christ's passion and resurrection are the one mystery for Christians and must always be celebrated as one, but on the *one feast* for which

Lent is above all a preparation. A congregation enjoined to rise with Christ in a common remembrance of its initiation into the body of Christ in baptism can scarcely do so if it has not reflected deeply on death and sin in the same context. There can be desperate reachings for Easter imagery in phrases like "deliverance from the deadly grip of winter," which will be meaningless on an Easter morning that is piercingly cold or in climates where winter and spring are equally mild. Not everywhere does nature come to life in April. Many Easter worshipers, besides, have given no thought to Lenten fasting or prayer. The rejoicing over new life to which they are invited on Easter Day will ring hollow if their Paschal liturgy is given only a resurrection character and not one of sorrow. The same will be true if they have come to worship on Palm Sunday as a genuine preparation for Christ's rising from the dead and have two-thirds of the Paschal *triduum* untimely thrust upon them in a reading of the passion and entombment. The Sunday that signals the final days of Lent must above all whet the appetite for coming to the assembly one week later to celebrate the sufferings of the one who left the Passover meal as a memorial of his death and an anticipation of his coming in glory. The celebration of his death and rising, which are in the profoundest sense ours as well, is a matter of the Great Night of Easter. Since the mid-fourth century it has seemingly become irreversibly a three-day observance. The final days of Lent introduce it. There is, therefore, not a seven-day liturgical observance from Palm Sunday to Holy Saturday called "Holy Week," only a popular designation of the time immediately preceding Easter.

Sunday of the Passion
Palm Sunday

Lutheran	Roman Catholic	Episcopal	Common Lectionary
Deut. 32:36–39	Isa. 50:4–7	Isa. 45:21–25 or Isa. 52:13—53:12	Isa. 50:4–9a
Phil. 2:5–11	Phil. 2:6–11	Phil. 2:5–11	Phil. 2:5–11
Luke 22:1—23:56 or Luke 23:1–49 (19:28–40)	Luke 22:14—23:56 or Luke 23:1–49 (19:28–40)	Luke (22:39–71) 23:1–49 (50–56) (19:28–40)	Luke 22:14—23:56 or Luke 23:1–49 (19:28–40)

SECOND LESSON: PHILIPPIANS 2:5–11

True to the suggestion made above, the first and primary look will be taken at the hymn which Saint Paul quotes as part of his exhortation to the Philippians in praise of the total mystery of redemption. He wants them to avoid selfishness and conceit, pursuing humility in each other's regard with the "incentive of love" which is Christ. Today's feast sets the tone for the Lent which is about to end on Thursday and the Paschal *triduum* about to begin on Friday. As to the first, there is Paul's plea to the community at Philippi that they all be "of the same mind, having the same love, being in full accord [*sympsychoi*] and of one mind." (2:2). He is clearly nervous, as he writes from prison (1:13), about the envy, rivalry, and partisanship (1:15, 17) which characterize some in the community. He does not want any to be intimidated by a threat of persecution of the kind he is being subjected to (see 1:27–29). Paul's plea for unity of spirit surely took hold two centuries later, for it was this that would bring Lent into existence: a feeling of fellowship with adult candidates for baptism, which led to the adoption of penitential dress and fasting by the long-baptized in the final six or eight weeks of preparation of the catechumens about to be baptized.

This community solidarity is uppermost in Paul's mind as he proposes the humility that counts others better than oneself as the only proper stance of those in Christ (2:2–3). Just as Lent arose as a kind of churchwide retreat to signal the entry of new Christians into the community, so the reckoning of the interests of others as totally on a par with one's own (2:4) was the primitive Christian spirit.

Paul cannot propose a better exemplar for the conduct of believers than the Christ Jesus who, as a slave, humbled himself to the depths of death on a cross. The response of God to this obedience was the exaltation of Jesus to the point where his name would be glorified throughout the three-level universe of the ancient world and his Lordship everywhere proclaimed (2:7–11). Basic to Paul's incorporation of this christological hymn is the use to which he puts it. It is not merely a faith statement of a pre-Pauline church, although it is that. It is for Paul a *paraklesis* or encouraging appeal to "have this mind among yourselves, which is yours in Christ Jesus" (2:5). Paul knew well that the mystery of human redemption could be set at nought if no believers were to pattern themselves on the self-emptying of Jesus (2:7), being content to confess in confident tones that he is Lord. Paul gave no evidence in his letters of having known the gospel tradition of Jesus' being hailed in triumph as he entered Jerusalem for the last time. Paul would certainly have recognized this reception as prophetic in the biblical sense. He would at the same time have deplored a triumphalist approach to the exaltation of Christ if it were not preceded by a lifetime of "humility, count[ing] others better than yourselves" (2:3), in effect a long Lent of mutual regard and service.

The present age is a difficult one in this matter. Any North American likely to be at a Palm Sunday service has grown up in a culture that has maimed some persons beyond the possibility of esteeming their own self-worth correctly. Others have been driven to view themselves as the center of the universe. Paul wrote his letters to a normal, virtuous/sinful population, guilty of great wrongs but capable of repentance. Such people still abound in Christian assemblies but they are surrounded by others who have been insulated against the possibility of "do[ing] nothing from selfishness or conceit . . . in humility count[ing] others better than [them]selves" (2:3). The great bulk of Palm Sunday Christians are present in the unspoken hope that something of the embers of the Spirit's warmth will be stirred in them as the Great Week comes on. They deserve every effort on their behalf to this end. They may have done little about the penitential season until now but it is not too late. The bruised heart and the contrite spirit are the great penances of the Christian. Compared with them, Compostellian pilgrimages and bodily fastings are empty exercises. The self-abasement of the follower of Christ, which consists in obeying God to the point of personal humiliation, is within the grasp of most who assemble to pray. They can and must be exhorted to it on this day if the next Sunday, Easter, is to have any Christ-meaning for them. Preachers need to ask the three-person'd God to "batter their hearts" to make the impending Paschal season profitable for them. John Donne, who wrote the poetic line above, did a Meditation on sickness unto death (numbered XVII) in which he caught exactly the self-emptying which Paul invites all to share with Christ. The phrase "No man is an island, entire of itself" appears here but we quote a few less well known phrases:

> The church is catholic, universal, so are all her actions; all that she does belongs to all. When she baptizes a child, that action concerns me; for that child is thereby connected to that body which is my head too, and ingrafted into that body whereof I am a member. And when she buries a man, that action concerns me: all mankind is of one author, and is one volume; when one man dies, one chapter is not torn out of the book but translated into a better language. . . .[10]

Donne could not have maintained that with any certainty if he did not first believe that God had highly exalted the obedient Christ Jesus, the servant of all, and bestowed on him the name above every name. The glorification of all in a heavenly Easter is a possibility if all, like Jesus, have spent a life in the service of all.

The hymn (Phil. 2:6–11) can be dealt with exegetically in a brief space. It has a three-stage christology. Christ first exists in glory, not as Johannine Word but as heavenly Adam (2:6). He sets aside that status by human birth, exchanging his God-like form *(morphē)* for a human form (2:8). It is not clear why the term "image" *(eikōn)* from the LXX (Gen. 1:26) is not used, as "likeness" is (Gen. 1:26; see Phil. 2:7). In the third stage, because of his obedience Jesus Christ is restored to glory (2:9–10). This is a picture of a Jesus who does not hold fast to his prerogatives but gives them up in the interests of servanthood, a role in which he is completely effective and for which he receives fitting praise.

Many doctrinal constructions have been placed on this piece of holy rhetoric which perhaps neither its first author nor Paul meant it to bear. The basic difficulty comes from the assumption that the hymn is rooted in a *Logos* christology. This makes the emptying of the fullness of deity by the Word an insoluble problem. Something similar is true of the wrestling over the meaning of *harpagmon:* He "did not count equality with God a thing to be grasped" (2:6). That uncommon and puzzling word "grasped" has to do with either laying hold of booty or having a stroke of good luck. Clearly it means somehow renouncing a uniquely advantageous position to adopt a posture of service. The humbling spoken of does not consist of a Johannine incarnation but of voluntarily serving others to the point of death without any assurance that vindication will follow. Nothing in the hymn suggests Jesus' knowledge of a divine restoration. Paul uses a song long familiar to him to insist that one must honor others by becoming their servant. Without this the mystery of Christ's death and resurrection may be celebrated but never understood. Grasping for status and power, Paul says, results only in loss and failure. The Palm Sunday homily that is serious will call for a deliberate disavowal of the self if the next days are to be significant as a reenactment of the mystery by which we are saved.

GOSPEL: LUKE 19:28–40

Joseph Fitzmyer in his definitive commentary, *The Gospel according to Luke*,[11] characterizes Jesus' entry into Jerusalem (Luke 19:28–40) as the beginning of the fifth of seven parts into which he divides this Gospel, after the prologue of 1:1–4. The pericope begins with the sixth mention of Jesus' journeying to Jerusalem (Luke 19:28; see 9:51; 13:22; 17:11; 18:31; 19:11), the entry into which had been announced at 13:35. The greater part of the narrative is derived from Mark (11:1–10). It embodies the tradition of Jesus' coming into the city from the east (Luke 19:29), probably in the company of a group of pilgrims who are greeted (19:38) with the phrase of benediction from Ps. 118:26. His coming on a colt about which he knows beforehand, as in Mark, does not include reference to Zech. 9:9. Matthew and John make explicit use of the prophetic passage in which a king enters victorious but humble on the foal of an ass. Luke seems to avoid consciously Mark's reference to the coming kingdom of David (Mark 11:10), contenting himself with having the crowds call Jesus "the King" who comes in the name of the Lord (Luke 19:38a). They also repeat the phrase about peace—here "in heaven," not on earth—from the song of the angels at Jesus' birth (19:38b = 2:14).

Commenting on Luke 19:28–40, it is important to ask whether in the minds of Jesus' contemporaries his entry into Jerusalem had any messianic connotations. That is almost impossible to answer. As early as Mark's Gospel and possibly his source, the "kingdom of our father David that is coming" (Mark 11:10) had been coupled with a greeting addressed to Jesus "who comes in the name of the Lord" (Mark 11:9). Luke's substitution of the title "King" (19:38) for the hailing of the coming kingdom may be his way of deflecting expectations that the kingdom will arrive soon (see 19:11) and putting in its place a Jesus—

no less regal—who is the "coming one" to the Lord's temple of Mal. 3:1 (see Luke 19:45). The question of the delegation from the Baptist about Jesus' identity is answered (Luke 7:19). The days "for him to be received up" (9:51) have arrived. To the whole story about Jesus a pronouncement story has been attached. The Pharisees resist the clamor of his disciples that accompanies his entry into the city, to which he replies: "I tell you, if these were silent, the very stones would cry out" (19:40). He arrives as a non-eschatological, non-political sovereign who will bring the peace of heaven, and so he *must* be hailed. The paradoxical nature of his kingship will come to light within the next days (see 22:25–27; 23:2–3, 37–38).

The Lukan "Palm Sunday gospel" has the same twofold theme as the Philippians hymn, abasement joined to exaltation. The difference is that the exaltation is anticipated by Luke despite the fact that he knows of the humiliations in store for Jesus (see 18:32–33). But the rejoicing of modern congregations will fittingly match that of the Jerusalem disciples because they know the joyous outcome of the days that are upon them. It is impossible on this day not to know that the forces of evil have been met and have been overcome. Julian of Norwich (d. after 1416) put it succinctly in her *Showings:*

> God gives joy freely as it pleases him, and sometimes he allows us to be in sorrow, and both come from his love. (Ch. IX, short text) . . . "If you are satisfied," our Lord said, "I am satisfied. It is a joy and a bliss and an endless delight for me, that ever I suffered my Passion for you for if I could suffer more I would." . . . "This deed and this work for our salvation were as well done as he could devise it." (Ch. XII) . . . "Since I have set right the greatest of harms, it is my will that you should know through this that I shall set right everything which is less." (Ch. XIV)[12]

The joy of Easter lies ahead but first there must be

> the Passion of our Lord as comfort to us against [the purging pain caused by our sins]. . . . He comforts readily and sweetly with his words, and says: But all will be well, and every kind of thing will be well. (Ch. XIII)[13]

Julian makes the denial of all our inward affections that are not good the condition of righting the frightful imbalance caused by sin. Contrition and acknowledgment of sin, to which one can only be led by the Holy Spirit, is the necessity of the coming days if all is to be made well in us by a suffering and rising Christ.

As to Luke 23 alone or Luke 22—23, we repeat the suggestion not to proclaim it as the gospel portion today but the Lukan entry of

Jesus into the city. For those homilists who feel bound by tradition or rubric, the following notes on the passion story in Luke may be helpful.

The climax of Jesus' departure (*exodos*, 9:31), to be accomplished at Jerusalem, comes when he prepares his disciples for it as the hour of the Passover meal arrives (22:14). Fitzmyer calls chapters 22—23 the sixth major part of Luke's Gospel. In it, Luke provides fourteen of the eighteen episodes of Mark in almost the same order, employing similar theological and apologetic motifs. The narrative is highly colored by these concerns and is at almost no point to be taken as factual reporting. The general charge of sedition against Jesus underlies 23:2 but the specific accusations are probably Luke's doing to prepare the reader for the exchange that follows. The prohibition of giving tribute to Caesar is palpably false (see 20:25) and the claim to be a king prepares the reader for Jesus' *titlos* (superscription) on the cross (23:38). Jesus' condemnation by Pilate is surely an authentic reminiscence (23:24) but not necessarily in response to a demand of "the chief priests and the rulers and the people" (23:13). Their collusion is a more apt term than is demand. The hortatory character of the passion narratives is uppermost, hence congregations are rightly asked to identify if they can with the innocent sufferer Jesus. One's state of mind and state of heart in the face of unjust persecution are much more to the fore for the evangelists than is consideration of what actually happened to Jesus in his last hours. Such details are not likely to have been known to them as reported, or indeed at all. The passion narratives were a tissue woven largely from biblical sources to bring home vividly to their first hearers the response they should make in similar circumstances.

Luke's passion narrative is marked by these characteristics in particular: an inimical Jerusalem leadership—which will conspire against Jesus (22:2)—as distinguished from the "people" or the "crowd" (22:2, 6 [NEB]; 23:27, 35, 48); Satan rather than the Roman or temple soldiery as primarily responsible for his betrayal and capture (22:3, 31), successful over him as "the power of darkness" (22:53; the Roman soldiers appear for the first time only in 23:36); Jesus' serene facing of death as what the Father wills for him (22:37, 39–46), but not alone, as in Mark—rather, he is comforted along the way (23:38) and even at the end (23:49); Jesus as an innocent (23:41) and just (23:47) sufferer who dies willingly (22:42, 51); the invitation to hearers to recognize their own weakness with Peter and their own malice with all who have condemned Jesus, while having a part in his patience and his mercy toward his captors and executioners (see 22:54—23:43).

Luke calls the upcoming feast of Passover *(pesaḥ)* by its Greek name *pascha* (22:1). Christian popular etymology within a century was joining it to the verb *paschein (pathein),* to "suffer" or "endure," although the words are not related. In the Quartodeciman struggle, recall that some wanted the resurrection to continue to be celebrated on the first day of *pesaḥ.* The term "Paschaltide" thus received a wider extension than both the Jewish feast and the idea of suffering.

Luke's first thirteen verses of chapter 22 are a discussion of preparations for the meal. Verses 14–38 describe preliminary activities, while 22:39—23:56 are devoted to passion, death, and burial. Of special interest concerning the meal are the textually disputed verses 22:19cd–20 (see RSV up to 1972), which the negative decision of Westcott and Hort,[14] compounded by Rudolf Bultmann's[15] view of 22:19–20 in their entirety, eliminated as being an interpolation. These verses have been restored by most critical editions and translations as textually authentic. Verse 18 is not a vow of abstention like Mark 14:25 but a simple statement that in light of Jesus' imminent sufferings this is his last meal with his friends until the banquet in the kingdom (see Luke 13:29).

It has been much disputed whether a true Passover meal is being described here. The weight of opinion favors a tentative yes (Joachim Jeremias is not at all tentative),[16] but the liturgical practice of the churches of Matthew, Mark, Luke, and Paul predominates in the accounts, leaving the actual occurrence including Jesus' words on the occasion unsure. The two cups of Luke (22:17, 20) are sometimes taken as evidence of what we know from later Jewish sources about four at the Passover meal, but the breaking and distribution of bread (22:19) would characterize any Jewish meal. The identification of the bread and wine with Jesus' body given and covenant blood poured out shows the reconciling nature of his sacrifice. The injunction to do as Jesus does as a memorial of him (22:19), not found in Mark or Matthew, is paralleled twice in 1 Cor. 11:24 and 25. This detail is indicative of Luke's possession of a meal-and-passion-source other than Mark which often contains touches found in Paul's and John's accounts. There is an affirmation of the disciples in Luke 22:28 such as Mark never makes, while the next two verses (29–30; cf. Matt. 19:28) are a Q-saying about their role as judges in the end time. Jesus' prayerful injunction to Simon to strengthen the others after he has a

change of heart (Luke 22:32) is unique to this Gospel. The impatient
dismissal by the "Lord" of a literal interpretation of his sword-saying
(22:36, 38; cf. 49–51) is enough to ensure its figurative character as he
speaks to his disciples of the challenges that will face them
(22:35–37). Luke's comforting angel while Jesus' sweats as if there
were "great drops of blood" (22:44) is an example of his powerful
narrative technique.

In Luke Jesus has a questioning before Herod Antipas, the tetrarch
of Galilee and Perea, which is not found in the other Gospels
(23:8–12). It could have been a genuine historical remembrance.
Herod's longstanding desire to see Jesus is fulfilled (23:8; cf. 9:9). He
evidently finds no reason to condemn this subject of his and returns
him to Pilate (23:11), the second Palestinian authority to find him
innocent of any crime, capital or otherwise (23:4, 14–15, 22). The
passages just cited constitute a threefold declaration of Jesus' innocence by Pilate which is in direct contrast to the antagonism of the
"chief priests and the rulers and the people" (23:13) found throughout chapters 22—23. It is part of the tendency in all the Gospels to
exculpate Pilate and place the blame on the Jewish leadership. This
was probably done out of apologetic motives, as much to underscore
Jesus' total innocence as to avoid imperial censure in the latter first
century. We know from Josephus the total disinterest of the high
priesthood in religion and its sycophantic relation with Rome necessary in order to continue in power. If modern congregations have the
Lukan narrative read to them they need to know how little solid
history they are hearing on this point and how strong an echo it is of a
polemic against the Jewish priestly leadership that had lost nothing in
sixty years of telling.

After the several stories that Luke recounts in 23:26–43, the narrative of Jesus' death is startlingly brief (23:44–46). Prodigies in
nature attend his passing. The centurion makes him innocent (23:47;
dikaios, a Jewish "just one"), a summing up of all that Luke had
wished to say of him.

FIRST LESSON: DEUTERONOMY 32:36–39; ISAIAH 45:21–25; ISAIAH 50:4–7, 4–9a; AND ISAIAH 52:13—53:12

As Deuteronomy comes to a close it incorporates two extended
poems which make up the bulk of chapter 32 and all of 33. It is from
the first of these, a review of Israel's history couched as praise of the

Lord its faithful protector, that the first reading in the Lutheran lectionary is taken (Deut. 32:36–39). Israel's infidelities and idolatries sadden the Lord, who would have given up on Israel long ago but for the anticipated taunt of its enemies that they had triumphed over Israel's God (32:27). Recompense and vindication will be in God's hands (32:35) when the power of Israel's enemies is spent (32:36). They have no rock like the Rock which is the Lord; their libations poured out to no-gods are powerless (32:38). Then comes the passage which determines why the Paschal liturgy employs it. Verse 39 describes the Lord as the God who authors death and life, woe and weal. What follows is on the bloody and vengeful side, in the manner of ancient Semitic writing. The point that underlies the Paschal mystery, however, has been made: the God of all human laying low and raising up is the one who will vindicate the obedient Christ. By his resurrection the enemies of God will be vanquished, chiefly sin and death and hell. These will be the captives whose blood will be drawn (32:42). God's vindication is an expiation. The land that believers will dwell in on Easter Day is one purged of their guilt (32:43). There is none that can deliver them out of God's hand. Already, one week before the saving events are commemorated, the work of deliverance is set in motion.

The first Episcopal reading of the two proposed (Isa. 45:21–25) makes the same point as the Deuteronomy passage: there is no god besides the Lord, righteous and a Savior (Isa. 45:21). The irrevocable oath that God has taken will be quoted by the Philippians hymn (2:10–11): "To me every knee shall bow, / every tongue shall swear" (Isa. 45:23). In Christian faith it is spoken of Jesus crucified who will be raised up as the Christ of glory in whom believers in the resurrection—"all the offspring of Israel"—shall triumph and glory (Isa. 45:25). The Roman and Common Lectionary selection (Isa. 50:4–7, 4–9a), while featuring a teacher of God's Word whose teaching gives sustenance and who because he does not rebel suffers for the flintlike set of his determined face, praises the God of vindication who stands near him (Isa. 50:4–7/9a). In the Episcopal alternative (Isa. 52:13—53:12), the prospering of the Lord's servant, so recently marred but now raised up, astonishes all. The first three verses set the Paschal tone but the long portion of chapter 53 places Good Friday squarely in the midst of a Palm Sunday congregation. God will vindicate the Jewish people and, as Christians are convinced, its great one Jesus, but this day is not the day of his suffering. This day remembers his anticipated vindication as he entered Jerusalem on a beast of derision, the ass's colt of Zech. 9:9 (as Matthew and John make out the simple "colt" of Luke to be).

The Gospels never tell us quite *how* the sufferings of Jesus reverse completely his fortunes and ours, only *that* they do. The Philippians hymn provides an answer. Jesus was not spurred by selfishness or conceit in anything he did. In humility he counted everyone better than himself in the sense that they were worth dying for. He knew that God would make it right somehow. That is what he always taught. And he lived by what he taught, up to the end. A homily on hosannas sounding in the ears of Jesus—this Jew who trusted God completely—on the brink of his dissolution might be the most powerful parable out of life that could be shared this day.

Monday in Holy Week

Lutheran	Roman Catholic	Episcopal	Common Lectionary
Isa. 42:1–9	Isa. 42:1–7	Isa. 42:1–9	Isa. 42:1–9
Heb. 9:11–15		Heb. 11:39—12:3	Heb. 9:11–15
John 12:1–11	John 12:1–11	John 12:1–11 or Mark 14:3–9	John 12:1–11

The faithful Christians who come out to pray publicly on this second day of the church's Great Week are worthy of the homilist's best efforts. There may be redundancy in the readings of the various communions as they are viewed horizontally but there is none as any one of the lectionaries proceeds vertically through the week. In the quiet of a weekday either early in the morning or in the evening after a day in the home or workplace—perhaps at midday in churches near office buildings in the city—there is the opportunity to explore, however briefly, the riches of the Bible. Helping worshipers understand how the early church read its Scriptures is a good beginning. Modern lectionaries, like ancient ones, proceed on the same principle as the New Testament books themselves. Faith in Christ Risen who had died in shame as an "evildoer" (John 18:30) sent those who believed in him to their sacred scrolls. These would disclose the painful paradox if anything could. And so it proved to be.

Prophecy in its day is the work of public-spirited teachers admonishing their contemporaries to read the signs of the times. They tell them to interpret the day's events from the long-term perspective which they are convinced is God's; to behave as if contemporary history were an insistent word of the Lord. True prophets never lack self-confidence. Their warnings go unheeded, they say, to the people's peril. Years or centuries later, prophecy becomes the work of another set of teachers. They explore the record of the past and tell what it meant *then* that speaks to the events of *now*. No expositor of Scripture's depths, therefore, should say simplistically, "As Isaiah wrote of Jesus eight centuries before his birth," but, "As Matthew [or whoever it might be] read Isaiah with faith in Jesus Christ, saying . . ." Prophecy works something like that old question from basic lectures on the physics of sound: "If there is no ear in the forest to hear it, is there a crash when the tree falls?" Those who made Isaiah's Servant Songs to *be* prophecy are the believers in Jesus Christ who find him there. Without the prescient pen of an early writer who saw Israel's role to be one of suffering if it persevered in its calling, there could have been no identification of Jesus as the paradigm of his people's suffering. Jews who have no special interest in the story of Jesus find an affront in this interpretation of their Scriptures. But it should be remembered that neither they nor the Christians find the Righteous Teacher in the prophets as the Qumranites did long ago. Prophecy is, quite literally, in the eye of the beholder.

FIRST LESSON: ISAIAH 42:1-9

There is a Servant Song (Isa. 42:1-4) and its response (42:5-9) addressed to the community in exile in Babylon ("Jacob" or "Israel") among the twenty-two poems of the first nine chapters of Second Isaiah (40—55). The major theme of these poems is the promise of return to the homeland, with passages of comfort, rebuke, plea, or charge and admonition freely interwoven. In the first of the Servant Songs of Second Isaiah (there will be four) employed here in the last days of Lent, a "chosen" one who enjoys God's favor—an individual? the people as a people?—will receive the charismatic "spirit" which impels to bringing forth "justice" (42:1). This does not seem to come as the result of a judging function over the nations so much as it is a matter of the entire Israelite revelation, beginning with the patriarchs and culminating in the Sinai covenant. The Servant must bring the Lord's self-disclosure to Israel to bear on the lives of the pagans. The justice of which the Servant is the intermediary is identical with the "law" or instruction of 42:4. The Syrian and Phoenician shores of the Mediterranean, the "coastlands," must learn of the revelation to Israel. Nothing is to dissuade the Servant from his calling to promulgate this message which brings peace. Stridency is not to be his way: not the loud proclamation of public authority nor the violence associated with the officers of a military regime. The poor and oppressed are not to have yet another burden placed on them by the rich and powerful. Israel's revelation is a way of persuasion yielding peace. Shared calmly but forcefully (see 48:1), it will "faithfully bring forth justice" (42:3). The message is not to be brought to Israel, note, but to the nations. The scope of salvation is thus broadened. Second Isaiah throughout goes beyond the confines of Israel to a larger world.

In 42:5–9 the Lord "responds" to the poem, repeating some of its phrasing and making its meaning more explicit. God speaks as the author of nature in the Job-like fashion of the passage above, 40:12–31, where "breath" and "spirit" are the principle of life for the whole animal kingdom. "If you take away their breath [your creatures] perish. . . . When you send forth your Spirit, they are created; and you renew the face of the earth" (Ps. 104:29–30, NAB). Yet the breath and spirit of Isa. 42:5 seem to do more than enliven creaturehood. They have made Israel "a covenant to the people, a light to the nations," thereby establishing the mission of the Servant as one as broad as humanity itself (42:6). The spread of Israel's revelation should mean an end to the blindness and captivity, both literal and figurative, which idolatry and injustice bring. The Servant is being designated a liberator, one who will be guided by the hand and protected (see 42:6) as had been promised in 41:10. The God of Israel proclaims the uniqueness which attaches to the name Yahweh and says that when the predictions just made come to pass, as others have before, Israel and the nations will be assured of their divine source. Poem and response together affirm in a way new to the Bible that the Lord is supreme over all the nations, not just over Israel. There is a plan afoot, this author says, which will involve the Gentiles fully. Israel as Servant will somehow be its agent or intermediary.

There is little wonder that Luke in his Gospel, which is so clearly dedicated to tracing the gift given to Jews as something to be shared with non-Jews, should put on the lips of old Simeon the following description of impending "salvation" (Luke 2:30): "A light for revelation to the Gentiles, and for glory to thy people Israel" (Luke 2:32). He repeats it twice in the Book of Acts, attributing the phrase from Isa. 49:6 (cf. 42:6) first to Paul and Barnabas (Acts 13:47), then to Paul (Luke 26:23). The gospel is to be given to Israel first and afterward to the Gentiles whom it has the historic calling to illumine. A church which has as its faith that Jesus is the son of Israel through whom law and justice are brought to the Gentile world does right to proclaim this passage on the brink of its Paschal observance. The church sees in the Spirit-filled, gentle Servant a type of Jesus upon whom the Spirit of the Lord rested (Luke 4:18), one who gave sight to the blind (4:18; 7:22) and came to set captives free (4:18).

He did not cry out to his tormentors or judges that a gross injustice was being perpetrated on him. One single remonstrance is reported of him (John 18:23). The evangelists identified him through a voice from heaven at his baptism as God's beloved Son in whom God was well pleased (see Luke 3:22). The whole story of Jesus and about Jesus is, for those who believe in him, a set of "new things I now declare" (Isa. 42:9). Whether they come to pass or not depends on two things: Will God deliver from his extremity this persecuted Jew who is the perfect type of Israel, a victim because of his Servanthood? And, if God should do so by raising him up, will a whole progeny live to validate the Isaian prophecy (see Rom. 6:3–11)? The Christians of the ages bear a heavy burden in responding to the second part of that question. The penitential season about to close and the three days of rejoicing about to begin contain the answer to it. The Servant is rightly proclaimed as the foreshadower of Jesus if believers in him as the Christ of God bring forth justice to the nations, doing all in their power to establish it on the earth. The candidates for public office they vote for, the opposition they mount to oppression at home or abroad, the struggle they engage in to make peace will be the proof of this. Jesus like the mysterious Servant was a protester in his way. Those baptized in him must be such in theirs.

SECOND LESSON: HEBREWS 9:11–15

The major doctrinal theme of Hebrews is priesthood and how Jesus by his sacrifice fulfills the office of the levitical priest perfectly. The Christian author does not engage in an allegorical exposition of the details of temple worship as Philo and Josephus do. Writing respectively before and after the temple's destruction, they found symbolic meaning in the veil of the temple, the seven-branched candlestick, the altar of incense, and so on. Hebrews largely contents itself with comparing the person and sacrifice of Jesus as "apostle and high priest of our confession" (Heb. 3:1) to that of the temple priesthood in an overall way, that is, in the act of sacrifice, not by a comparison of details. The first ten verses of chapter 9 are devoted to a contrast of the two covenants as they are concerned with the prescriptions of public worship, the details being chiefly those of the tent in the desert derived from Exodus 25—26. At Heb. 9:7 the theme of blood is rather offhandedly introduced, surprising since it will figure so prominently in the treatise. The author relies on biblical data for his description. He need not have had firsthand experience of the temple liturgy. He allows himself one allegorical detail ("symbolic," v. 9, for which the word employed is *parabolē*). It is this: so long as an outer tent and an inner one exist, with all the preparations necessary to prepare gifts and sacrifices on this side of the separating curtain, the lack of free passage and the need of a once-yearly passing through it for atonement purposes symbolizes the old eon. But in Jeremiah's speaking of a new covenant which will render the first one obsolete (see Heb. 8:13), the author finds support for the idea that a new order or reform impends to supplant a scheme which cannot affect persons' inner lives but only rectify their ritual offenses (Heb. 9:9–10).

Jesus as the antitype of temple sacrifice is developed succinctly in today's second reading of the Lutheran and Common Lectionaries (Heb. 9:11–15). The differences in, first, the place and form of worship are spelled out in vv. 11–14, and, second, those between the two covenants they stand for ("first" and "renewed," au. trans.) in v. 15. Jesus is called the "high priest of the good things that have come" (v. 11), showing the preference of the RSV for the textual reading *genomenōn*. Even if *mellontōn* ("to come") were in the original text, the difference would not be great. By his appearing a new age is inaugurated which is laden with benefits. The "greater and more perfect tent (not made by hands . . .)" of v. 11 (see 8:2, "the true tent") is the heavenly sanctuary. Christ enters into it bringing his own blood, not that of goats and bulls (9:13). He is "without blemish" (9:14), which is the necessary condition of the slaughtered animals. He offered himself "through the eternal Spirit" (v. 14; or "in his eternal nature," as Hugh Montefiore renders it).[17] However it is translated, the phrase conveys that which is divine in him. His blood achieved an inner benefit of immense proportions for a covenanted people, not just one in the area of ritual impurity. The Christian who hears a passage such as this read out loud must realize that the author of Hebrews who could be a Jew—Apollos of Corinth is the candidate of some—is not impugning ritual as such but praising the greater liturgy that God has achieved in Christ. He has been made the mediator of a "new" covenant (*diathēkēs kainēs*, v. 15). This is better translated "renewed," since Jeremiah and Ezekiel did not contemplate the revocation of the Sinai covenant in the future but its more faithful observance. Those called to be parties to it have a "promised inheritance" available to them.

Homilists on the first day of the Great Week may choose to preach on this reading alone if it occurs in their lectionary. This would be a marvelous readying for the celebration of the boon of redemption in the upcoming *triduum paschale* provided that preachers do no denigrating of the cult which their own Scriptures describe as divine ordinances. Hebrews, like Paul, had nothing against the Judaism contemporary with them—certainly not against the religion of Israel *which they professed*—except that it was not Christ. This epistle is a symphony in praise of "how much the more": the new thing God had done in Jesus Christ lately. The cross and resurrection are being praised, not the temple liturgy dispraised. As the reading proposed by the Episcopal Lectionary puts it (Heb. 11:39—12:3), the people of great faith in Israel "did not receive what was promised, since God had foreseen something better for us" (11:39–40). Their perfection, the writer goes on, depends on Jesus' endurance of the cross, in the face of which we may not grow weary or fainthearted (12:3).

GOSPEL: JOHN 12:1–11; AND MARK 14:3–9

The evangelist John probably knows of an anointing of Jesus at Bethany from the tradition which would also contain the dating in 12:1, an otherwise insignificant detail (see Mark 14:3–9 = Matt. 26:6–13; Luke 7:36–50; the latter seems to be related to and has several features in common with John's account). The story is laid in the village but not the household of the family with which Jesus is friendly. The remark of John 12:2 links the family up with chapter 11, while 12:3 appears to have been the beginning of the story before the linking sentence was inserted. John's identification of Mary of Bethany as the central figure—in Matthew and Mark she is "the woman"—coupled with Luke's description of a woman guilty of many

sins (Luke 7:47) has resulted in the popular conflation of this Mary
with the sinful woman and Mary Magdalene. But no Gospel speaks of
the Magdalene as sinful; Luke alone says that "seven demons had
gone out" from her (8:2 [a pathological statement?]; Mark 16:9
makes it Jesus who "cast them out").

The proximity to the Passover in John creates the special suitability
of the reading for this week. Its importance to John and to the
church's liturgy is christological. Judas Iscariot is rebuked for his
concern over Mary's waste of ointment, and hence money, by Jesus'
remark connecting Mary's generosity with his impending death. In
Mark Jesus challenges even more explicitly the indignant "some" who
object. There he proposes that she be allowed to keep the nard "for
the day of my burial" (John 12:7). Mark has Jesus say, "She has
anointed my body beforehand for burying" (14:8). The quotation
from Deuteronomy 15:11, given in the Gospel as "The poor you
always have with you" (John 12:8), has nothing callous about it as it
does on the lips of people who know neither Deuteronomy nor John.
In context the verse continues: "Therefore I command you, You shall
open wide your hand to your brother, to the needy and to the poor, in
the land" (Deut. 15:11). As all the evangelists but Luke employ it, the
verse highlights the uniqueness of this time and this person about to
die.

John probably found the story in this form in the tradition, not in
Mark, with the names already attached (the designation "Judas Iscariot" is not characteristic of him). It fitted his christological purpose
perfectly. He was able to edit it slightly with additions like "he who
was to betray him" (John 12:4) and the imputing of theft to Judas as
his motive (12:6; see 13:29 for reiteration of Judas's being in charge of
the common fund). In fact, however, Mark 14:11 and Matt. 26:15 also
accuse Judas of avarice. Mary's generous action is far from wasteful in
John's eyes but is the best possible use of such costly ointment. The
concluding verses (12:9–11) are John's editorializing. Much of the
interest of the Judean crowd is curiosity but some genuine belief in
Jesus comes of it (12:9, 11), an indication that not all the "Jews" of
John, whatever the term may mean, are portrayed as hostile to him.

The Gospel uses the gathering of the crowd at Bethany as a further
reason impelling the "chief priests" to plot Jesus' death and that of
Lazarus as well (12:11; cf. 11:53). This is the normal suspicion people
in power have of gatherings they cannot account for. It should be
remembered, however, that John had made an unwitting prophet of

Caiaphas when he spoke of "gather[ing] into one the children of God who are scattered abroad" (11:52), so that very little is to be taken as the history of Jesus' last days. All is symbol, a much more powerful language than fact with which to convey to us the portentousness of these events. When the figurative term "ransom price" is employed to describe a death which will affect all who ever have lived or will live, we know that only the language of type or sign can convey to us the magnitude of the reality. All Scripture is symbol, whatever pericope the homilist may choose to preach on. Exegesis may help to shed light on a few puzzling details but it is the faith of the church in the significance of these events that has given meaning to this book of symbols before the homilist begins to speak.

Tuesday in Holy Week

Lutheran	Roman Catholic	Episcopal	Common Lectionary
Isa. 49:1–6	Isa. 49:1–6	Isa. 49:1–6	Isa. 49:1–7
1 Cor. 1:18–25		1 Cor. 1:18–31	1 Cor. 1:18–31
John 12:20–36	John 13:21–33, 36–38	John 12:37–38, 42–50 or Mark 11:15–19	John 12:20–36

FIRST LESSON: ISAIAH 49:1–6;
AND ISAIAH 49:1–7

Jeremiah of Anathoth was known to the Lord before he was formed in the womb (Jer. 1:5), like the Servant of this second poem and, well after them, both the Baptist and Jesus. All had a work to do that was of divine initiation. Such is the meaning of their naming by name (Isa. 49:1) or consecration (Jer. 1:5). Since all election by the Lord is equally mysterious and can only be alleged in terms of outcome, the church is faithful to the laws of prophecy in seeing a type of Christ in the Servant in light of the faith it has in what was accomplished through this son of Israel. Only in this song, of the four (see Monday's first reading; today's; 50:4–9a; and 52:13—53:12), is the Servant designated by name ("Israel," 49:3). A mouth "like a sharp sword" (49:2) means words of power, not cutting or bitter speech. Similarly, the hiddenness of the Servant is figured doubly as something in the shadow of God's hand or in a quiver. Rabbinic thought sees here the unknown identity of the Messiah. The Servant addresses the people of the "coastlands" (49:1; cf. 42:4; 41:5–10) as the westernmost point imaginable to a people in eastern exile who, as an offspring of Abraham (41:8), originally came from there. The Servant claims that through him the Lord will receive the glory that is due the God of Israel (49:3). The meaning of 49:4 is a puzzle: Does Israel reflect here on its unsuccessful efforts of past centuries to glorify the Lord properly? Perhaps the reference is to the warnings of the prophets which went unheeded. But the speaker's "right" and "recompense" indicate the vindication he hopes for in the future. And they are spoken of in a tone of confidence. To gather Israel, to bring Jacob back to the Lord, is no small thing but the Servant is sure he will accomplish it. Honor and strength are his from God (v. 5). What more can he ask for? His calling is to bring light to the nations, the Lord's salvation to the ends of the earth (v. 6).

Jesus, whom the liturgy sees prefigured here, did not in fact have founding a church as part of his calling. That was not necessary because he already belonged to one—God's unique assembly *(qahal)*, Israel. His mission was to gather it from among the Gentiles where it was scattered and to restore it to its earliest beauty. The outcome is well known. Non-Jews came streaming to this Israel, as the Second and Third Isaiah had prophesied would be the case in the final days. The Gentiles came to bask in the light of "the preserved of Israel" in its restored condition (v. 6). The salvation of Israel's God finally reached them. All this is told in muted fashion but v. 7 makes explicit the promise the Holy One of Israel holds out to a despised and abhorred people. This is probably why the Common Lectionary adds it. In type, the people, which is the slave to rulers, will have kings and rulers prostrate themselves before it. In antitype, the Paschal victim, held contemptible by his tormentors, will be venerated by a multitude when his chosenness is revealed in the resurrection. The Servant as vindicated sufferer is one whom the church does right to turn to in its preparation for Paschaltide. Without Jewish suffering, it needs to ask itself, could there have been a redemption of the kind it hails? Without this Servant people and its centuries of readying for a mystery that would touch the lives of many outside its confines, how would anyone know what to make of Jesus at his appearing? Israel and he are absolutely correlative, as every Christian worshiper should know.

SECOND LESSON: 1 CORINTHIANS 1:18–31

Desiderius Erasmus, that Augustinian canon whom no monastery could hold (though he always got the permissions he needed from his superiors for his petulant wanderings), wrote a satirical Latin treatise to which he gave the Greek title *Morias Egkomion,* "The Praise of Folly." He dedicated it to his English friend Thomas More, saying that "your name is as close to the Greek for folly as you are far from the meaning of the word." Erasmus chatters on for 150 pages on the foibles of monks and friars, theologians, and the human race in general. The reader may by this time write him off as a shallow if witty moralist—not humorous, but extremely penetrating—only to come upon the most refreshing anthology of all the praise of folly to be found in Scripture. Today's reading from 1 Corinthians is the centerpiece, of course, but the Psalms and the prophets are there and above all Jesus in the Gospels.

> But Christ seems to take his greatest delight in little children, women and fishermen, while the dumb animals who gave him the greatest pleasure were those furthest removed from cleverness and cunning. So he preferred to ride a donkey, though had he chosen he could safely have been mounted on a lion; and the Holy Spirit descended in the form of a dove, not of an eagle or a hawk, while throughout the Scriptures there is frequent mention of harts, young mules and lambs. Moreover, he calls those who are destined for eternal life his sheep, though there is no animal more stupid [says Aristotle]. Yet Christ declares himself the shepherd of this flock and even takes delight in having John point him out as "The Lamb of God." . . . The apostles whom he chose were simple and ignorant and to them he unfailingly preached folly. He taught them to shun wisdom and made his appeal through the example of children, lilies, mustard-seed and humble sparrows, all foolish, senseless things, which live their lives by natural instinct, free from care or purpose. . . . Then perhaps we shouldn't overlook the argument that folly finds favor in heaven because it alone is granted forgiveness of sins, whereas nothing is forgiven wisdom.[18]

Paul seemed to know a crowd in Corinth that was capable of every human folly. His attempt to steer them toward God's foolishness and away from their own wisdom is a classic example of truth couched in paradox. "God has chosen what the world counts folly" (1 Cor. 1:27, NEB) and "It pleased God through the folly of what we preach to save those who believe" (1 Cor. 1:21) are foundation stones of Paul's gospel.

The season of utter foolishness in the Christian calendar is just days away. Haranguing Jews and Greeks—in the dichotomy of Paul's Jewish world there was no one else—is an old homiletic game. The trouble is that makes it sound as if preachers and their hearers had somehow escaped the flood tide of folly. The fact is that the cross is a stumbling block to any Christian within earshot of any other. It should do no harm to proclaim this loudly in these closing days of Lent. The silly season is upon us—God's silly season—and suddenly everyone turns sober. G. K. Chesterton said of last Sunday's donkey that he was

> The devil's walking parody
> On all four-footed things.

But, "tatter'd outlaw of the earth, / Of ancient crooked will" that he was, he had the last laugh.

> Fools! For I also had my hour;
> One far fierce hour and sweet:
> There was a shout about my ears,
> And palms before my feet.[19]

This most foolish of beasts knows real fools when he sees them, assembled in this church as we are.

GOSPEL: JOHN 12:20–36

Who were the Greeks *(hellēnes)* who came up to Jesus and why does John tell of them? As so often in this Gospel they are foils who will elicit a response from Jesus predicting his ending (John 12:30–33), a prophecy given as threefold in the Synoptic Gospels. His death will be his glorification, his defeat his victory. These Greeks have come "to worship at the feast" (12:20) but this does not make them Diaspora Hellenist Jews. They are more likely to be ethnic Gentiles at some stage of adherence to Jewish morality and practice. The "Greeks" appear in only one other passage in the Fourth Gospel, at 7:35. In both places they probably stand for the outreach to the non-Jewish world (as do the Samaritans of ch. 4), which John knows is a reality of his time but does not feature in his Gospel. He may be dependent on a source for this anecdote and insert mention of them here—attending to them no further—to remind his readers that "seeing Jesus" (see 12:9), always a term in John for viewing in belief, will not be confined to Israel once Jesus is "lifted up from the earth" (12:32). At that point he will draw "all" (*pantas,* male and female) to himself.

Philip and Andrew, the two disciples with Greek names, may be known to John for having evangelized non-Jews. In any case the Greeks' request speaks of an inquiry into the Gospel outside the ranks of Israel. Important in the pericope for preaching at the end of Lent is Jesus' nonresponse of 12:23–26, which indicates that the saving gospel cannot be proclaimed to the Greeks or anyone else until Jesus dies and goes into the earth to bear much fruit. Neither can it be received unless the hearers do the same ("hate [their lives]," v. 25). Like master like servant, John seems to say. It is the prediction of Mark 8:31 put another way, but even more so of Mark 8:35 and its parallels, with John 12:26 at the same time a clear echo of Mark 10:45. Being in the service of Jesus is following him to his death, which will end in the heavenly world to which he goes (see John 14:2–3). The figure of a grain of wheat going into the earth was a rabbinic commonplace to describe the resurrection of the just (see also 1 Cor. 15:37). Whoever wishes to give thought to anticipating Christ's glory on the Easter which is in prospect must do some dying to self in the waning days of the penitential season. The mystery of dying and rising is one for this evangelist in his double-edged phrase, "[being] lifted up from the earth." So it is for the church. Shame and glory are two sides of the same coin. Jesus cannot regain the glory which he had before the world was made (see John 17:5) without death and burial. No more can his followers (12:26), but in their case it is death to the disobedience which is sin that is required.

Schnackenburg calls vv. 23–28, "the Johannine 'Mount of Olives.' "[20] The "hour" of Jesus' glorification (see 12:23; 17:1) must be preceded by the painful one from which he asks the Father to be saved. It is the hour predicted in 2:4 and fulfilled in 19:27. In its element of suffering this hour will be reproduced in the lives of disciples (see 16:4). Jesus' prayer to God that the Father's name be glorified is parallel to the first petition of the Lord's Prayer (Matt. 6:9; Luke 11:2). The answer given by a heavenly voice is identified by the crowd in its John-induced state of confusion as thunder—apocalyptic speech for the voice of God—or the voice of an angel (cf. Luke 22:43). This is John's assurance to the reader of the glorification of Jesus by the Father (12:28) with a glory which he in turn gives to God (cf. 13:31–32 found in the Catholic Lectionary for today). The confirmation is for the crowd's sake, not for his, Jesus says (12:30), and he proceeds immediately to speak of his being raised up from the earth as an act of judgment on the world and its ruler. By this judgment is meant punishment for unbelief in him as crucified and risen, whereas believing in him as Son of man will mean the attraction of all to him (12:31–32). This causes confusion. Is not the Messiah's reign to be lasting? For John, the evil one is already defeated by the onset of Jesus' hour. His death is the twofold elevation already known to the evangelist which stands as the symbol of acceptance or nonacceptance of Jesus as the light. Darkness is the fate of any who will not believe in him. To be of the light is to know that he is a Christ who must die.

There is ample food for reflection here for weekday worshipers. They hope to avoid judgment by the events they are about to contemplate, proceeding rather into the light. They believe in a Son of man who had to depart from the world in pain yet who, upon being lifted up in glory, will remain forever. The Paschal option is set before them: "Behold, I set before you light and darkness. Choose light!"

The proposed Episcopal gospel readings (John 12:37–38, 42–50) are in the same vein as 12:20–36 commented on above. The saying or the word that Jesus spoke will act as judge on the last day. Since he spoke only as the Father bade him, it was as if the people had heard from his lips the Father's commandment which is eternal life (see 12:44–50). The account of the cleansing of the temple in Mark (11:15–19) is situated in that Gospel as if it took place in Jesus' last days, and as having triggered the plot to be rid of him out of fear.

Wednesday in Holy Week

Lutheran	Roman Catholic	Episcopal	Common Lectionary
Isa. 50:4–9a	Isa. 50:4–9	Isa. 50:4–9a	Isa. 50:4–9a
Rom. 5:6–11		Heb. 9:11–15, 24–28	Heb. 12:1–3
Matt. 26:14–25	Matt. 26:14–25	John 13:21–35 or Matt. 26:1–5, 14–25	John 13:21–30

FIRST LESSON: ISAIAH 50:4–9a

On Monday and Tuesday the first two Isaian Servant Songs were read and now the third. In Isa. 49:7 in the first of a series of Zion poems the people of Jerusalem have been spoken of as "deeply despised, abhorred by the nations, the servant of rulers." None of the world's great ones can see how this mean instrument Israel will be used by God for a mysterious saving purpose which will touch the lives of all. Zion demurs, saying that the Lord has forsaken her (49:14), but is told that her oppressors shall bow down to her and lick the dust of her feet (49:23). The Servant now speaks (50:4–9), with vv. 10–11 as the response to the song. He tells of the hardships he experiences in exercising his prophetic calling ("the tongue . . . a word . . . opened my ear," 50:4–5). He nets a series of humiliations for his pains as a teacher, not unlike the indignities heaped on Jesus held captive (v. 6). The face the Servant would not hide he set like flint (v. 7), like the determined jut of jaw ascribed to Jesus as he proceeded toward Jerusalem (see Luke 9:51). The Servant is sure he will not suffer ultimate humiliation at the hands of unbelievers who will not heed him—here not the nations, it seems, but fellow Israelites—because he knows the Lord will vindicate him (Isa. 50:8a, 9a). He throws down the challenge that he should be met in a court of law much as the Lord has done (see 41:21; 43:9), in proposing that arguments and witnesses be summoned and the case be brought to judgment: "Who will contend with me? . . . Who is my adversary? . . . Who will declare me guilty?" The Christian who preaches on or hears these words at this season inevitably thinks of Jesus as the sustainer of those who are weary with a word. His voice is about to be stilled. But not before he summons his adversaries to the judgment of darkness that overtakes disciples who will not walk in the light. Jesus is no rebel but rather one who relies on God as his vindicator. Like the Servant he suffers setbacks that seem to be a divine judgment on him whereas, in fact, it is sin whose measure is being taken.

SECOND LESSON: ROMANS 5:6–11

The figure of a law court as the place where the innocent may find justice, which the Second Isaiah favors, is resorted to by Saint Paul. Among his many images of what Christ's death achieved (reconciliation, expiation, life), justification is perhaps the best remembered in the West, as sanctification is in the East. All of these benefits are available in this life for Paul. Salvation alone—an end-time concept—he reserves for the age to come (see Rom. 5:9, 10). He accepts the tradition he has received of the blood of Christ's sacrifice as an expiatory sign like the blood on the doorposts in Egypt or the mercy seat in annual atonement. Paul develops this symbolism in a legal direction, making the blood of Christ that which justifies at law (sets right, acquits). It did so at a point when we were beyond any doubt guilty ("yet sinners," 5:8). Justification, a present reality, was achieved in Paul's immediate past. Enmity with God has been replaced by reconciliation. As a result there lies ahead deliverance from the divine wrath (v. 9). Rejoicing in God through Jesus Christ is the fitting response, in light of our present reconciled state (v. 11).

This neat summary of what Christ's obedient death achieves for a church that believes in it sets the tone for the days ahead. The three-day liturgy will be celebrated by a people reconciled. All in this company are sinners; some are egregious sinners. It would be folly to say, however, that even though cosmic sin is long overcome that enmity with God is completely a thing of the past. All of Lent was a season of repentance for the sins committed after baptism. The sacrifice of Christ justified us but we are characteristically halfhearted in availing ourselves of the new, justified state it holds out to us. These are fitting days to consider what our reconciliation means. If reconciliation comes with faith in the death of God's Son and salvation by his life, the final consummation will surely be imperiled if the proferred being-at-one with God is accepted lukewarmly. Pardon for unforgiven sin is certainly required. This is as much a part of the Christian tradition as the Jewish. Why is it that Paul so deemphasizes repentance, referring to it only once as the condition of forgiveness (2 Cor. 12:21)? The probable answer is that transgressions leading to guilt did not figure in his thoughts as much as did the basic deliverance from bondage to personified sin.

The celebration of the institution of the Lord's Supper impends— itself a reconciling ordinance. Some churches have rites of private forgiveness and penance conducted publicly at this season. These go back to the days of Polycarp of Smyrna (d. 156) who wrote to the Philippians that it was the presbyters' task to "bring back compassionately those who had wandered" (6.1). We only begin to know the details of early penitential practices from a writer like Tertullian (d. after 220) in *On Penance*. The footwashing of Maundy Thursday liturgies affords the opportunity for the appropriate expression of sorrow for sins of omission of the service that is due. The upcoming *triduum* cannot, in any case, be entered upon overconfidently as if, because we are reconciled to God in Christ, there were no need for a bruised heart and a contrite spirit. The fact that Paul does not deal theoretically with sins which incur guilt, aside from charging people to avoid them because they are incompatible with life in the Spirit, does not give Christians the liberty of basking in their justified state as if they could come to no harm. He was well acquainted with the danger of slipping back into old ways and warned against it frequently. Because possession of the Spirit was the highest value for Paul—a confirmation of the transfer from bondage to sin to the Lordship of Christ—he made this the supreme value to which repentance and forgiveness were subordinate. But repentance for the "quarreling, jealousy, anger, . . . gossip . . . [and] impurity" the Corinthians had practiced was very much his expectation (2 Cor. 12:20–21).

The Episcopal reading from Hebrews was commented on largely under the Common Lectionary on Monday. The latter's proposal of Heb. 12:1–3 today anticipates Easter joy as Jesus' endurance of the cross is proposed as the model of Christian perseverance.

GOSPEL: MATTHEW 26:1–5, 14–25; AND JOHN 13:21–35

The Lutheran and Catholic Lectionaries read Matt. 26:14–25 today, the Episcopal also proposing it preceded by 26:1–5, the plot of the chief priests and elders to arrest Jesus, as the alternative to John 13:21–35 which is the favored reading (largely the Catholic gospel selection for yesterday). The Common Lectionary gospel, John 13:21–30, is an abbreviated version of the John 13 pericope.

On Monday the Episcopal Lectionary named Mark 14:3–9 as the alternate reading, the pouring of ointment on Jesus' head by a woman in the house of Simon the leper. Matthew follows Mark closely in this passage (Matt. 26:6–13) and continues to do so in today's gospel reading, 26:14–25 (= Mark 14:10–21). Matthew's chief editorial change is to develop the story of Judas's bargaining with the chief priests (Matt. 26:15) and add his question to Jesus, "Is it I, Master?" eliciting the response, "You have said so" (26:25). The account of the betrayer's tragic death will also be added (27:3–10). It is not certain why Matthew develops the story of the traitor's price so fully. Judas's venality was evidently part of the tradition (they "promised to give him money," Mark 14:11). Matthew with his penchant for citing biblical texts to show fulfillment in Christ probably gravitated toward Zech. 11:4–17, an allegory about a good shepherd who received a slave's wages (thirty silver shekels; see Exod. 21:32) which he threw back into the temple treasury. This is the first of many quotations in the passion account. Matthew will return to the silver pieces by way of Jeremiah in 27:3–10. Judas, meanwhile, looks for a chance to betray

Jesus (26:16). Judas's "opportunity" and Jesus' "time" (26:18) are closely cognate Greek words.

Matthew eliminates Mark's story of the man carrying the water jar as a guide to a large upper room and turns the disciples' question about the room's location into an authoritative statement: "I will keep the passover at your house with my disciples" (26:18). He predicts his betrayal by one of them. All are distressed, asking, "Is it I, Lord?" (26:22; a title found seventy-nine times in Matthew), and Jesus then gives the sign of the hand dipped in the dish (v. 23; see Ps. 41:9). No bread is mentioned in the Gospels as it is in the psalm, although John will speak of a "sop" or "morsel" (John 13:26, KJV and RSV respectively). The Mark/Matthew tradition has Jesus say that the Son of man must go his providentially determined way; further, it were better for Judas had he not been born (Matt. 26:24). The latter sentiment is a judgment passed by the tradition which has led to endless speculation about the divine foreknowledge and Judas's eternal outcome. Probably no statement on either question was intended; instead it is only an expression of profound regret at the parting of friends. The judgment is evidently too harsh for Luke, who omits it. Finally, Matthew alone has Judas put the question to Jesus which all had asked about the betrayer's identity (26:25). He does not have Judas call him "Lord" but "Rabbi" (RSV, "Master"), a title denoting hostility or distancing in this Gospel. The "You have said so" is both acknowledgment and judgment, a stance which Matthew does not shrink from.

Where should homiletic emphasis fall in this richly set table of readings? Probably on the Servant's determined decision to have it out with his adversaries, for which the dogged persistence of Jesus despite the treachery of a friend is a good match. Speculation on Judas's state of mind should be avoided since all the narratives are literary constructs about friendship betrayed that are built on the barest reminiscence. In fact, the Romans text may be the most inviting of all because Jesus dies for Judas among others, the most evident "sinner" and estranged one on the gospel scene. If the possibility of Judas's being justified and ultimately saved is not allowed, then the paradox of Christ's dying for the ungodly has little meaning (Rom. 5:6). It is something to consider.

Maundy Thursday

Lutheran	Roman Catholic	Episcopal	Common Lectionary
Jer. 31:31–34	Exod. 12:1–8, 11–14	Exod. 12:1–14a	Jer. 31:31–34
Heb. 10:15–39	1 Cor. 11:23–26	1 Cor. 11:23–26 (27–32)	Heb. 10:16–25
Luke 22:7–20	John 13:1–15	John 13:1–15 or Luke 22:14–30	Luke 22:7–20

We have been speaking throughout these pages as if Maundy Thursday might be thought a day of the *triduum sacrum*. It has become such popularly with the passage of time but anciently it was not so. It was long the last day of Lent. Saint Augustine spoke of the *triduum* of the One crucified, buried and upraised, meaning the three days of suffering, resting in the tomb, and resurrection—the latter extending over fifty days until the commemoration of the Spirit's descent. The Easter celebration was conceived as commemorating predominantly the Lord's death which was a pathway to the resurrection. The resurrection came to receive the chief emphasis but it always contained the remembrance of the passion which preceded it. The earliest forty-day fast in preparation for this *triduum* ran from the first Sunday of Lent, *Quadragesima,* to Holy Thursday inclusive (the reckoning of weekdays only as Lent was to succeed it). Thursday was the day of reconciliation of public sinners, including their readmission to the Eucharist.

A fast of forty hours preliminary to Easter is among other prevalent periods mentioned by Irenaeus in the late second century (see Eusebius's *History of the Church* V.24.12). This was evidently a pious vigil preliminary to the feast. Which forty hours were observed, however, we cannot be sure. From Jesus' death and entombment at three o'clock on Friday to seven o'clock on Sunday morning is one possibility; some other distribution over the two days is the other. Augustine speaks of forty hours as being the length of time Jesus was under the dominion of death (*On the Trinity* IV.6).

By the fourteenth century the Easter Mass was being celebrated as early as midday on Saturday. This means that the beginning of the forty hours of prayer before a replica of the holy sepulchre—a custom with early medieval, Frankish roots—was at eight o'clock on the "Evening of the Lord's Supper." A life of Saint Ulrich of Augsburg

(d. 973) by a certain Gerard tells of his placing of the Blessed
Sacrament along with the more commonly deposed crucifix in the
"sepulchre." He communicated the people on Good Friday and returned the Sacrament to its place of repose until Easter Day.[21] These
are the liturgical origins of what would later be termed erroneously
"the Mass of the pre-Sanctified," actually a communion service on
Good Friday which distributed to communicants the consecrated
hosts kept in a "repository" during the forty-hour period. Gregory
Dix places the ultimate origins of the practice in the second century
when people communicated at home on days the Eucharist was not
celebrated.[22]

On Thursday night, Egeria reported, the Offering (i.e., the Eucharist) was celebrated in the evening by the bishop in the Chapel
Behind the Cross, the only day of the year it happened; at it, all
communicated (35.2). This Eucharist was preceded by one at 2:00
P.M. The Jerusalem practice of a morning and evening celebration was
being resisted by Augustine toward the year 400 when returning
pilgrims pressed it on him (*Letters* 44.5). In Rome by 500 there were
evidently three Eucharists on Thursday: a morning one for the reconciliation of penitents in which that rite replaced the eucharistic rite,
another at midday for the consecration of the holy oil *(chrisma),* and a
third in the evening to commemorate the Last Supper. The ceremony
of footwashing at this evening Eucharist was introduced by Gallo-
Frankish reformers such as Theodulf, bishop of Orléans (d. 821), the
same ones who introduced from the East practices like the Palm
Sunday procession, the Veneration of the Cross on Good Friday, and
such major elements of the Easter Vigil as the Blessing of the New
Fire and the hymn *Exsultet* sung to Christ in the symbol of the Paschal
candle.

The term "Maundy" is what Norman French made of Jesus' word in
the Vulgate at John 13:34, *Mandatum novum do vobis,* "A new
commandment I give to you." In earlier times the day was called
simply "the Fifth Day (Thursday) of the Lord's Supper." It is to the
readings for a day with such a checkered history that we now turn.

FIRST LESSON: JEREMIAH 31:31–34; AND EXODUS 12:1–14a

Chapters 30—33 of the Book of Jeremiah are often called "The
Book of Consolation."[23] The first two chapters are mostly in poetry
and the second two entirely in prose. In the first half Israel (called

"Jacob" and meaning the northern kingdom) is promised rescue from its despoiler Assyria. John Bright, in his commentary on Jeremiah, thinks it not impossible that the promise of a ruler "com[ing] forth from their midst" (30:21) may have been written by Jeremiah himself of Judah after the exile.[24] The restoration of the north, Israel or Ephraim, called here a "remnant" (31:7), will come first (v. 8). This probably means, at the very least, that in chapters 30 and 31 we have authentic sayings of Jeremiah which were delivered in Josiah's reign (622-609). Rachel, weeping in Ramah (a passage especially familiar to Christians through Matthew's use of it as a symbol of unmitigated grief; 2:18), is told rather to restrain her tears because her sons, deported to Assyria, will come back from the enemy's land (Jer. 31:16). The material in these chapters gives hope for the future: virgin Israel will return to her cities (31:21), to Judah and its people—no doubt an addition made after the Babylonian deportation of 587— where the holy hill Zion stands (vv. 23–24).

Three prose portions of chapter 31 are introduced by the formula "Behold, the days are coming, says the Lord" (vv. 27, 31, and 38). The first now makes of the Lord, who before had plucked up and destroyed, a builder and a planter (v. 28). The third describes in detail the rebuilding of Jerusalem's walls (vv. 38–40). It is the second that constitutes today's first reading, the promise of a new covenant which the Lord will "cut"—the technical term—with both northern and southern kingdoms (v. 31). It is spoken of as unlike the covenant of Sinai (v. 32) but its description as "new" *(hadashah)* is better translated "renewed" since the Bible is insistent that the Lord's promise, once given, is irrevocable. The newness of the covenant is not the result of the Lord's change of mind but of Israel's infidelity to it (v. 32), spoken of under the figure of a broken marriage first used by Hosea (chs. 1—3) and by Jeremiah earlier in this book (ch. 3). The substance of the promise is the interiorizing of the terms of the covenant: the Lord will inscribe the covenant in human hearts (Jer. 31:33). In that future day the teaching of neighbor by neighbor will be needless because the divine forgiveness of sin will have as its chief effect that those destined to be God's people (v. 33) will know the Lord (v. 34).

With the symbolic remembering of the "new covenant in my blood" as today's observance (see Luke 22:20; 1 Cor. 11:25), homilists need to be wary of the claims they make of the fulfillment of the Jeremian prophecy in the church. The author of Hebrews in retrospect appears premature in the vocabulary he chooses to describe an obsolete or aging covenant that is "ready to vanish away" (Heb. 8:13). A resistance to the terms of the new covenant by Christians over the ages should incline those who speak for them, and to them, to recall that only in Christ has the promise been fulfilled. As inaugurator of the final age Christ alone needs no teacher of the law; it is inscribed in his heart. Even those who accept the sealing of the new covenant in his blood (see Heb. 9:14, 26; 10:10) with strong faith are conscious of how far they fall short of the self-offering of the high priest who is also perfect victim. Believers in the Paschal mystery are acutely conscious of the new covenant held out to them. They need to be reminded constantly of their failure to fulfill its terms. Only Jesus has accepted these terms wholeheartedly in his obedience to God (Heb. 10:9–10). Stress on the "already" of human redemption in the person of Christ is important. Its full measure from our side, however, is very much a "not yet." In a word, the Easter triumph is his in fact but ours only in hope.

The Roman Catholic and Episcopal first reading on Maundy Thursday is the Exodus instruction on preparation for the Passover meal. This was employed on Good Friday from medieval times (Exod. 12:1–11). It is here lengthened to v. 14 and the Passover lamb given the Johannine typology of Jesus as servant (John 13:1–5; cf. 1:29) rather than as eucharistic food. The restoration of the footwashing in the recent liturgical reform undoubtedly accounts for this. Important to observe is the incorporation of the postexilic Passover observance into a narrative purporting to be historical. It is actually a ritual account, a description of the family meal to be kept forever as "a memorial" (*le zikkaron*, Exod. 12:14). This phrase becomes in translation the *eis tēn emēn anamnēsin* of the eucharistic liturgies of Luke (22:19) and Paul (1 Cor. 11:24).

Another caution to homilists will keep them from describing Exodus 12 as identical with the Jewish *seder* ("order") since, as with Christian liturgies, numerous details of the modern *haggadah* (here, "ritual tradition") were added to the prescriptions of the Mishnah (Pesaḥim, 10; ca. 200) in the Middle Ages—above all the replacement of a lamb by a piece of bone because of the temple's destruction. Ancient Israel and Christianity have in common blood as the sign of redemption, a daubing of it as the symbol of life or a wine-red cup—both to convey the reality of life. Jewish rite and Christian sacrament are parent and child. No adaptation of pagan mystery religions, such as the "history of religions school" demands, is needed to account for the meal that saw body and blood in bread and wine. Saint Paul came upon the practice already alive in the tradition when he first came to believe.

SECOND LESSON: HEBREWS 10:15–39; HEBREWS 10:16–25; AND 1 CORINTHIANS 11:23–26 (27–32)

Again the lectionary tradition is twofold. Our first consideration will be of the Lutheran reading, Heb. 10:15–39 (followed by the Common, Heb. 10:16–25), then of the Catholic/Episcopal selection (1 Cor. 11:23–26 [27–32]). On Monday of this week the Lutheran and Common Lectionaries employed Heb. 9:11–15. It appears in the Episcopal two days later with five verses appended, 24–28 (see pp. 27–29, 39 above). The Episcopal, meanwhile, had Heb. 11:39—12:3 on Monday; the Common used the last three verses on Wednesday. All the pericopes from Hebrews are much alike because the book has a single theme: the superiority of Jesus' sacrifice to that of the temple because his calling as mediator of the new covenant is higher. Details may differ but the "something better [God has foreseen] for us" (Heb. 11:40) is that which is constant. In some passages like 12:1–3 Jesus is proposed as a model of endurance. Mostly, however, his once-for-all sacrifice of himself at the end of the age (9:26) is contrasted favorably with the limitations attending the annual sacrifice of goats and calves.

The Maundy Thursday selection at its longest (Lutheran) begins with the quotation of Jer. 31:33–34 from the first reading. It concludes that no further offering for sin is needed once there has been forgiveness (Heb. 10:18). But no one should think that Jesus' exercise of his office as high priest has taken away human responsibility. The stern warnings contained in the reading must be carefully attended to. The reading needs to be proclaimed slowly and carefully. If it is done well a commentary is almost unnecessary; if it is done badly the homily on it will be almost incomprehensible. In brief, the earliest hearers are being reminded of the hard struggle and abuse they had endured in the days after their enlightenment (i.e., their baptism) and the compassion that marked their first fervor (10:32–34). Deliberate sin after their earliest faith knowledge could turn the sacrificial act meant to remit sins into severest judgment (10:26–31). They are encouraged to persevere in faith, hope, love, and mutual encouragement to good works "as the Day draw[s] near" (10:22–25). The passage is a remarkable blending of faith as Paul preached it (10:22, 38, 29) and fear of punishment for consciously "profan[ing] the blood of the covenant" (10:29). Whoever preaches on this reading opts to underscore the perils of "spurn[ing] the Son of God." As great priest Jesus has seen to it that God will remember sins and misdeeds no longer. But equally present is the stern warning about setting at nought the mystery of redemption commemorated at this season.

Paradoxically, neither of the first two readings has a memorial-meal character as the gospel does. The theory of the framers must be that the new covenant that was promised need not be accepted. The Spirit of grace can be outraged (see Heb. 10:29). In such case the framers might have done better to continue the Lukan gospel reading as far as the woe directed by Jesus in Luke 22:22 to the one who would betray the Son of man. As it is, the reading ends at Luke 22:20.

The Catholic/Episcopal second reading (1 Cor. 11:23–26 [27–32]) recites the Christian meal tradition even as the first reading had provided the Jewish. There is thus coherence between them on the character of this day as the Last Supper observance. Paul's account of the tradition he received "from the Lord" (namely, the church) and delivered to the Corinthians is closest in wording to Luke among the Synoptics, in a passage the latter part of which will be commented on below. Both differ from the Mark/Matthew tradition in having Jesus' command over the bread, "Do this in remembrance of me" (1 Cor. 11:24; Luke 22:19). Only Paul will repeat it over the cup with the added phrase "as often as you drink it" (1 Cor. 11:25). He rehearses the tradition as a means of checking the factionalism that is tearing the community apart.

There was never a heresy about the Eucharist in the church's early centuries. It took the dispute over the views of Berengar of Tours (d. 1088) to bring the ninth-century struggle between sacramental symbolists represented by Ratramnus and physicalists by Radbertus into full light. The differences between Reformers and Catholics and even among the reforming giants on the modes of Christ's presence can be presumed to be well known to homilists in the various traditions. Saint Paul's problem was more fundamental: the utter betrayal of the "sacrament of love, sign of unity and bond of charity" (Augustine, *Tractatus in Ioannis Evangelium,* chap. 6, n. 13) by self-regarding, exclusivist behavior. The apostle recalls the tradition of a common meal in which the priest and victim of the new covenant—here, the language of Hebrews—is the very food and drink of those for whom it is promulgated. It is therefore entirely fitting to attend to mutual respect and affection in the community on this day, whether the footwashing or "maundy" is part of the rite or not. Whatever a congregation's theological convictions about the sacramental reality of the Lord's Supper, it may not turn either the meal or the footwashing into a "lying sign" by its failure to love. For Paul's phrase, "without discerning the body" (11:29), means precisely the failure to attend to community needs. "Eat[ing] and drink[ing] judgment upon" oneself (1 Cor. 11:29) is the "profan[ing] of the blood of the covenant" that Hebrews speaks of so sternly (Heb. 10:29). Christians are right to approach the Lord's table in the holy fear that they may do so while failing to love.

GOSPEL: LUKE 22:7–20

The first two Lutheran readings about the new covenant "after those days" (Jer. 31:33; Heb. 10:16) lead naturally to the Supper account in Luke which peaks in the "cup poured out for you [which] is the new covenant in my blood" (22:20). The third evangelist edits the details of the meal preparation he finds in Mark (Luke 22:7–14 = Mark 14:12–17), changing only the taking of the initiative from the disciples to Jesus and supplying the names of Peter and John as the ones sent. Jesus' foreknowledge of the unusual sight of a man carrying a jar comes from Mark. So does the identification of the Supper (never called the "Last Supper" in the New Testament, incidentally) as a Passover meal. Luke makes "the twelve" of Mark "the apostles" (the phrase "the twelve apostles" is a Lukan contribution), Matthew "the twelve disciples" (26:20). Luke 22:15–17 and 19cd–20 seem to come from a special Lukan source and not to be a reworking of Mark's material. Least of all is it the case that Mark's words of Jesus at the Supper table derive directly from 1 Corinthians.

Luke 22:19cd–20 which follow on Mark 14:22 have an interesting textual history. This so-called long text was considered an interpolation by Westcott and Hort in their critical edition of 1881. Their opinion was highly influential, resulting in the banishing of this verse and a half to the category of "other ancient authorities add" in earlier editions of the RSV. The editing of the early-third-century papyrus codex P[75] in 1961 confirmed the authenticity of the long text already found in the fourth-century Vaticanus and Sinaiticus, thus bringing to an end arguments on textual grounds against Luke's cup-bread-cup sequence.

Jesus' ardent desire to eat the Passover with his friends before he suffered (Luke 22:15) seems to be a wish fulfilled, not unfulfilled by his abstention from eating. "For . . . I shall not eat it again" (22:16) would translate the emphatic negative better, since the force of this verse and v. 18 is that the present Passover meal of lamb and bread and wine will find its eschatological fulfillment in "the kingdom of God." It is not only the past deliverance from Egypt that is being commemorated. Type will lead to the antitype of future and final deliverance. "Having received a cup and given thanks" (v. 17), in a fairly literal translation, is probably an echo of the first or second of the four Passover draughts. "Taking bread" (v. 19) as in Mark 14:22, Jesus "give[s] thanks" over it in the same formula as of 1 Cor. 11:24, rather than "uttering a blessing" (Matt. 26:29; Mark 14:22). The Luke/Paul vocabulary of thanks has resulted in the traditional designation "Eucharist"; it could have as easily gone the Matthew/Mark way, "Eulogy" or "Blessing." God is the one who is thanked/blessed for the gift of food which here signifies the future kingdom. The sharing of the cup preceding or following the bitter herbs and fruit compote *(haroseth)* led to the breaking and sharing by Jews of a small unleavened Passover loaf not unlike today's pita bread. This would characterize the beginning of any Jewish meal but the liturgical formulary betrays its Passover meal origins. The "cup after supper" would have been the "cup of blessing." Jesus' "body given" and "blood poured out" are "for you" (22:19, 20). Clearly Luke expresses an intention of vicarious offering here. The death of Jesus will be saving for others in its effect. The command to the disciples to do what Jesus has just done in memorial of him (v. 19d; not repeated over the cup as in 1 Cor. 11:25) is a directive to replace remembrance of departure from Egypt with unleavened bread (Deut. 16:3) by the bread and cup which will forever bring him among them. The Eucharist thus becomes the *seder* of Christians. Nothing other is needed than to celebrate it as a meal.

The climax of the passage is the cup as "new covenant in my blood" (Luke 22:20). The phrase surely preceded the appropriation of it by Luke and Paul. It is the capstone of any Holy Thursday homily on the Lutheran Lectionary readings. Covenant renewal in Jesus' blood is the central meaning of the Christian Pasch, hence, of the eucharistic meal.

The Catholic gospel and first Episcopal selection (John 13:1–15) occurs in the missal of Trent and comes from centuries before, reflecting the Maundy character of the feast. Jesus' act of love for "his own who were in the world" (John 13:1) needs little comment but his cryptic exchange in vv. 9–10 with Peter may. (For this see my volume *John*[25] where it is maintained with Schnackenburg[26] and others that "except for his feet" in v. 10 is the interpolation of a scribal literalist and that Peter's zealous request for bathing of hands and head is the introduction to a metaphorical statement of the kind in which this Gospel abounds.) The bathing that Jesus speaks of symbolizes participation with him in his impending death (see vv. 7–8). The disciples are already cleansed by their association with him (see 15:3). Their community with Jesus will be solidified by his death. Permitting him to serve them in this humbling way is identified by John as the sign of it.

Good Friday

Lutheran	Roman Catholic	Episcopal	Common Lectionary
Isa. 52:13—53:12 or Hos. 6:1–6	Isa. 52:13—53:12	Isa. 52:13—53:12 or Gen. 22:1–18 or Wisd. 2:1, 12–24	Isa. 52:13—53:12
Heb. 4:14–16; 5:7–9	Heb. 4:14–16; 5:7–9	Heb. 10:1–25	Heb. 4:14–16; 5:7–9
John 18:1—19:42 or John 19:17–30	John 18:1—19:42	John (18:1–40) 19:1–37	John 18:1—19:42 or John 19:17–30

FIRST LESSON: ISAIAH 52:13—53:12; AND HOSEA 6:1–6

The first reading chosen for the liturgy on the day of Jesus' death (Isa. 52:13—53:12) is generally reckoned to be the fourth and last of the "Servant of the Lord" oracles of the Second Isaiah. The others are 42:1–4 (in which the central figure is just, meek, and kinglike in bearing); 49:1–7; and 50:4–9a (in the latter two, the *'ebhed YHWH* acts like a prophet). The Lord's Servant will be "raised high and greatly exalted" (52:13, NAB) and "render kings speechless" (52:15,

NAB) despite a marred appearance (52:14) and lack of stately bearing (53:2).

Who is this stricken person—"spurned and avoided" (53:3, NAB)
"smitten by God, and afflicted" (53:4)? The humiliated one who will
be cut off (53:8) is probably the Jewish people in a state of "death" in
Babylonian exile at the time. Its growing up like a sapling out of the
parched earth before the Lord (53:2) would describe desert origins in
the days of the patriarchs. Suffering and infirmity, scorn at the hands
of powerful neighbors (53:3), was Israel's self-perception of its lot. Yet
this people, pierced and crushed, brought healing to many (53:5). "A
grave among the wicked" and "a burial place with evildoers" (53:9,
NAB) would be the living death of an exiled people among the
pagans of Babylon. But the acceptance of this fate as an offering for
sin can make many just and remove their guilt (53:11). A place
among the great and mighty will be the outcome—pardon for the sins
of many because of this Servant's obedient suffering (53:12).

It is remarkable how little of the wording in the passion narratives
can be traced to the Servant Songs, though much comes from the
Psalms and the prophetic writings. Silence before accusers, yes (Isa.
53:7), and buffeting and spitting (50:6), but these are generic. There
is nothing directly dependent on the Servant texts. Even when John
writes of Jesus' pierced side (John 19:37) he quotes Zech. 12:10 rather
than alluding to Isa. 53:5. The Mishnah is equally silent on these
poems describing a vindicated sufferer.

Egeria, visiting Jerusalem in the early 380s, says that the whole
time between noon and three on Friday "is taken up with readings.
They are all about the things Jesus suffered: first the psalms on this
subject, then the apostles [the Epistles or Acts] which concern it,
then passages from the Gospels. Thus they read the prophecies about
what the Lord would suffer, and the Gospels about what he did
suffer" (37.5).[27] Given the three-hour period, during which she says
the people weep constantly, it is almost unthinkable that the Servant
Songs would not have been read publicly. Two lectionaries from mid-
fifth-century Armenian Jerusalem show Isa. 52:13—53:12 as being
read at noon on Good Friday.

It is hard to know why the passion narratives did not use the
Servant Songs. Luke alone cites Isa. 53:12, he "was numbered with
the transgressors," just before Jesus went out to the Mount of Olives
(Luke 22:37). When Matthew employs Isa. 53:4 (citing Matt. 8:17) it
is as a proof text for Jesus' bearing our sufferings and enduring our

infirmities as he performed cures and exorcisms (Matt. 8:16). Luke in Acts 8:32–35 quotes Isa. 53:7–8 and applies the passage to Jesus. And 1 Peter 2:22–24 contains several implicit quotations in the sequence 53:9, 12, 5–6.

The church in its passion piety has certainly followed the lead of Acts in identifying Jesus with the Suffering Servant. This means above all that his disgrace and death are not paramount but his victory is: "See, my Servant shall prosper, he shall be raised high and greatly exalted" (Isa. 52:13, NAB).

The important point this reading makes is not the ways in which the Servant is brutalized but (as a note in the Oxford Annotated RSV puts it) "the numbed astonishment of the world's rulers" at God's exaltation of the "disfigured Servant (Israel)." Christ's upraising from the dead is in prospect for believers in the mystery of his death. To concentrate on its ignominy and its pain might obscure the glory that God means to bring from it. Jesus undoubtedly was an innocent sufferer but the greatness of his deed lay in his innocence, not his suffering. His submission to God's inscrutable will was the heart of his passion, not the blows struck by ignorant executioners.

Hosea 6:1–6, proposed as an alternative reading, has a long pre-Reformation history of being read on this day. The restoration promised for the third day accounts for its presence (6:2) but the continuation of the symbolism of the Lord as predatory lion from Hosea 5:14 relates to the feast commemorating Jesus' death. The God who has "torn" and "stricken" Ephraim and Judah like a desert wildcat is the one who will heal and bind it up. "He will revive us" (6:2) does not mean "raise from the dead" but "restore to health." The reference to the third day may be an echo of the reawakening of the dying fertility gods of Babylonia but it can as readily be a measured interval without specific origins. The Lord's restoration of Israel is as "sure as the dawn" (6:3), while the spring rains support the theory of a fertility rite as background. Verses 4–6 are the beginning of an extended oracle of the Lord. Here God's constancy is portrayed as the sun's light and Israel's inconstancy as the morning dew (v. 4), for it had the teachings of the prophets available to interpret its chastisements (v. 5). Formal religion represented by temple sacrifice is not the response the Lord expects; rather the Lord expects steadfast love and knowledge of God (v. 6). An entire theology of Jesus' self-offering is contained in anticipation in this eighth-century dialogue.

The brief reading from the Wisdom of Solomon suggested as an

Episcopal alternative (2:1, 12–24) was influential on the New Testament writers, like other parts of the deuterocanonical material. Wisdom 2:1 is a clear echo of Job 14:1 and 7:9. For Wisd. 2:13 see Matt. 27:43; John 8:55; 10:36–39. For Wisd. 2:14 see Matt. 9:4; while the idea of Jesus as a "just one" is found throughout the NT (see Matt. 27:19–24; Luke 23:47; Acts 3:14; 22:14; 1 Peter 3:18; 1 John 2:1, 29). Wisdom 2 is a classic place for the righteous man condemned to insult, torture, and death for his very righteousness (vv. 19–20).

SECOND LESSON: HEBREWS 5:7–9

Hebrews similarly portrays Jesus our great high priest as an innocent sufferer (5:7) who has passed through the heavens (4:14) and now has access to the throne of grace (4:16). This makes Good Friday a day of triumph for Jesus and us, not a day of unrelieved sorrow. The confession (*homologia*, v. 14) we hold fast to is belief in Jesus the Son of God and our high priest who can sympathize with our weaknesses because he was "in every respect . . . tempted as we are, yet without sin[ning]" (4:15). This natural sympathy of Jesus for those who are tested was featured in 2:18. He himself is "beset with weakness" (5:2), but in the universal faith of the NT he never consented to sin (cf. 2 Cor. 5:21; 1 Peter 2:22, quoting Isa. 53:9; Heb. 7:26). There is no passage in the gospels quite so graphic as this one (Heb. 5:7–9) to describe what Jesus endured in his passion.

If the temptation we are subject to means anything it means growing weary in the fray and feeling the pull of a wrong course of action as an attractive option. Jesus' will to serve God must have been constant. It was not untroubled, Hebrews says, but knew the lure of the opposite course. Our approach to the throne of grace, therefore, on this Friday we call "Good" is a confident search for "help in time of need" (4:16) from a victorious intercessor who will give that help.

The many musical settings of the passion for the poem *Stabat Mater* of Jacopone da Todi and the more ambitious compositions like the *St. John* and *St. Matthew Passion* of Bach will express human agony on this feast day—Christ's sufferings and ours. Many visionaries and prophets hang crucified today with Christ. Irrational and absurd suffering is all around us but so is much that is accountable and repented of. The tears of many parents are absorbed in the sorrow of Mary at the cross—whom the Gospel describes, however, only as "standing" there (John 19:25). The Magdalene was the weeper (John 20:11). It is right to wish to know that our suffering has reached the heart of God, who at the same time needs to know the measure of our faith in the victory of Christ over our suffering.

GOSPEL: JOHN 18:1—19:42

The passion narrative according to John is so vast a tapestry that only a few aspects can be featured in any homily based on it. It presents a Jesus who is fully aware of his own fate (18:4), before whom his would-be captors fall to the ground in dismay (18:6), and who magisterially instructs Pilate more than the prefect interrogates him (18:33–38; 19:9–11).

After Jesus' capture in a place familiar to Judas (18:2), Jesus is led "first" to Annas, who appears only here and without previous introduction (18:13). He is correctly identified as the father-in-law of Caiaphas, whom we know from Josephus to have been the high priest at the time. It was not an annual office, hence the phrase describing the son-in-law's tenure is probably to be translated "in that fateful year." John 11:46–57 seems to be a sentence of death passed on Jesus by Caiaphas or at least the sealing of his doom, which is plotted in this Gospel, as the narrative is crafted, from 5:18 onward. This may account for the relative brevity of the hearing before Annas ("the high priest"—18:19–24) and the suppression of any appearance before Caiaphas, the actual officeholder by dint of the older man's influence (18:24, 28).

Peter's cowardly denial (18:15–18) contrasts with Jesus' brave stand before his captors (18:5–8) and before Annas (18:19–23), as in the Synoptics. If the "other disciple" of v. 15 were the "disciple whom Jesus loved" (21:7) it would serve to authenticate the narrative, for the latter is described as the figure standing behind it (21:24). Attractive as the hypothesis of identity is, it cannot be proved. As to Jesus' response to the high priest regarding his "teaching" (the teaching of the Johannine community almost certainly), one gathers from it that the essential issues between Jesus and *hoi Ioudaioi* have already been debated and decided—chiefly in chapters 7—10—leaving Jesus' answer in 18:20–21 as John's summary of that situation.

The Roman trial before Pilate is markedly different from the Jewish hearing. It is a superb example of the evangelist's literary and theological genius and is not to be confused with the *genre* of history—apart from the fact that Pilate did sentence Jesus to death ("handed him over . . . to be crucified," 19:16). That *hoi Ioudaioi* ("to them") did it is impossible. The main interest is in the scenes where

Jesus and Pilate are alone on the stage: 18:33–38b and 19:9–12a.
There we find theological discussions on the nature of Jesus' kingship,
on truth (the Johannine *alētheia* which is the truth of God in Jesus
Christ, not philosophical truth), and authority from above—again,
not that granted by the Roman state but by God who is the chief
author of the drama.

Any pulpit treatment of this powerful narrative that sees in it a
history of Jesus' last hours misconceives it. An exploration of its
themes which sees them consistent with the entire Gospel that pre-
cedes is on the right track. A reading of the passion that recognizes it
as both cosmic and existential for Christian communities like John's
and the homilist's is dealing with it correctly. The "world"—all that is
set against God's truth in Jesus—is the sole enemy in the play, not
Judas or Pilate or Simon Peter or the crowd. Cosmic sin is pitted
against total innocence.

Francis Thompson caught the Johannine spirit well in "The Veteran
of Heaven," quoted here in part, which ends in a triumphant flourish
from Revelation:

'Twas on a day of rout they girded Me about,
    They wounded all My brow, and they smote Me through the side:
My hand held no sword when I met their armed horde,
    And the conqueror fell down, and the Conquered bruised his pride.

What is this, unheard before, that the Unarmed makes war,
    And the Slain hath the gain, and the Victor hath the rout?
What wars, then, are these, and what the enemies,
    Strange Chief, with the scars of Thy conquest trenched about?

The Prince I drove forth held the Mount of the North,
    Girt with the guards of flame that roll round the pole.
I drove him with My wars from all his fortress-stars,
    And the sea of death divided that My march might strike its goal. . . .

What is *Thy* Name? Oh, show—"My Name ye may not know;
    'Tis a going forth with banners, and a baring of much swords:
But My titles that are high, are they not upon My thigh?
    'King of Kings!' are the words, 'Lord of Lords!';
It is written 'King of Kings, Lord of Lords.' "[28]

Easter Vigil

Lutheran	Roman Catholic	Episcopal	Common Lectionary
Gen. 1:1—2:3	Gen. 1:1—2:2	Gen. 1:1—2:2	Gen. 1:1—2:2
Gen. 22:1–18	Gen. 22:1–18	Gen. 22:1–18	Gen. 22:1–18
Exod. 14:10—15:1	Exod. 14:15—15:1	Exod. 14:10—15:1	Exod. 14:10—15:1
Isa. 55:1–11	Isa. 55:1–11	Isa. 55:1–11	Isa. 55:1–11
Rom. 6:3–11	Rom. 6:3–11	Rom. 6:3–11	Rom. 6:3–11
Luke 24:1–11	Luke 24:1–12	Luke 24:1–10	Luke 24:1–12

When Egeria visited Jerusalem from Gaul or Spain she reported the Jerusalem liturgy in great detail because it was so new to her. It was new to everybody in the early 380s, having been devised by Bishop Cyril some thirty-odd years before. Only the Paschal Vigil was familiar to Egeria, which "they keep like us" (38.1).[29] Her eye for detail was remarkable but often she does not make a comment when we most wish she would: she tells us nothing of the Vigil readings.

Some of her omissions were made up for by the publication of two manuscript versions of the Armenian lectionary of Jerusalem from the early fifth century. The first manuscript was from the tenth century, the second from near the close of the twelfth, Armenian translations (it is supposed) from the Greek. The Armenian readings for the Vigil of Easter, each preceded by a part of Psalm 118 and each followed by the rubric "prayer with kneeling," are repeated here, in order to give modern homilists a sense of their link with the past:

Gen. 1:1—3:24   Job 38:1–28
Gen. 22:1–18   2 Kings 2:1–22
Exod. 12:1–24   Jer. 31:31–34
Jonah 1:1—4:11   Josh. 1:1–9
Exod. 14:24—15:21   Ezek. 37:1–14[30]
Isa. 60:1–13

After this came the recitation of Dan. 3:1–51 (the three young men in the fiery furnace) divided into two parts in the middle of v. 35. Only the two from Genesis and that from Exodus 14—15 have survived in our modern lectionaries. When the West had twelve readings from Hebrew Scripture at the Vigil (regrettably shunted to Saturday morning until recent reforms returned it to after midnight Saturday night), the pre-Reformation list included three more from fifth-century Armenian use: Ezek. 37:1–14; Exod. 12:1–12; and Dan. 3:1–24. In the reformed Roman rite there are now seven. In addition to those given under the heading "Good Friday" above, the fourth is Isa. 54:5–14, the sixth Bar. 3:9–15, 32—4:4, and the seventh Ezek. 36:16–28.

The rationale behind either of the longer sets of readings, Eastern or Western, has been preserved in the present set of four from the Hebrew Scriptures and two from the Christian. A brief story of salvation is summarized, although "deliverance" might be the better word. God creates a world and a human pair to be its stewards, calls into existence a covenanted people by whom all the nations of the earth shall bless themselves, delivers this people from bondage bringing them through the sea to dry land and offering an everlasting covenant to the repentant—both of those who claim David's kingship and of the Gentiles who neither knew Israel nor were known to it. The fulfillment of the promise comes with baptism into Christ's death and its symbolic burial with him. This brings a being alive to God in Christ as a pledge of the life with him that is to follow.

The Vigil is capped by the oblique challenge of the two men at the tomb to the women to report to the Eleven that the Son of man has risen on the third day. Remembering that the Vigil was connected with the initiation of new Christians from an early time, we are right to see in the readings the creation of the human couple in innocence, deliverance from the bondage of sin as through water, the wine and milk that were the new Christians' portion (see Hippolytus's *Apostolic Tradition* 23, ca. A.D. 215), the new life of those who emerged from the baptismal bath *(piscina)*.

It is unwise to attempt to comment in detail on all six readings. By the time of the homily the congregation is both weary from the length of the rite and in many places chilled from outdoor readings by firelight—yet whetted from some insights into all the Scripture they have heard. They should not be disappointed. Of greatest importance is to remind them of the sweep of history from the time when the earth was a "formless wasteland" down to reading from Luke about the Living One who like the newly baptized is not to be sought among the dead (Luke 24:5).

The marvelous Elohist prose-poem in praise of creation—presumably postexilic and culminating with the blessedness of the sabbath in Gen. 2:3 which all but the Lutheran Lectionary mysteriously omit—is followed by the account of the binding of Isaac and the reiterated promise to Abraham (cf. Gen. 12:2–3; 15:5) regarding all the families of the earth being blessed in his descendants. Israel's passage through the waters swept with a strong east wind (Exod. 14:21) and Egyptian horse and chariot cast into the sea (Exod. 15:1) come next. An Isaian promise of the Lord's fidelity follows: "So shall my word be that goes forth from my mouth; it shall not return to me empty, but it shall accomplish that which I purpose, and prosper in the thing for which I sent it" (Isa. 55:11).

The readings are the rising action in the drama of a world's salvation in Christ. Only the ancient convention of holding the reading from "the apostles" (i.e., the evangelists) until last keeps Luke 24:1–11 from providing the next reading after those from the Hebrew Scriptures, for surely the kerygma of Christ risen comes next in the history of redemption. Paul's reflection on its meaning should logically come last (Rom. 6:3–11).

All of the readings feature a baptismal motif, as was said, for such was the original reason for their choice: the primordial goodness of the world and all its creatures, the promise of future greatness to a people whose obedient father Abraham spared not his own son, deliverance from darkness and slavery as through water, an everlasting covenant of peace sealed through a life-bearing word, God's wisdom bestowed and God's wisdom abandoned, complete newness of being in a new land for people purified as by water.

The preparation is perfect for a reflection on being baptized into the death of Christ. For the people gathered on this holiest of nights is a people baptized, participating in the baptism of others. It knows its sinfulness in an old self crucified with Christ (Rom. 6:6) but still ready to assert itself rebelliously against God. The sinful body is destroyed and the slavery is over *for those who have died with Christ.*

Christ alone is raised up from the tomb in glory: "Death has no more power over him" (Rom. 6:9, NAB). If his life is life for God so must ours be. We must consider, regard, think of ourselves only as dead to sin as he is, and as alive to God in this same Jesus Christ. This is the faith outcome in us of the creation-redemption-sanctification deed that is all one to the God who did it on our behalf.

> The strife is o'er, the battle done;
> Now is the Victor's triumph won;
> Now be the song of praise begun, Alleluia!

This is the night, a Great Night indeed, a sacramental reliving of all that a God of mercy has done for us. The Scripture readings are summed up in this hymn of praise *Exsultet* to a redeeming God through the obedient death and resurrection of the Son:

Rejoice, you hosts of heaven, rejoice, all you who participate in the divine mysteries! Let trumpets sound the triumph of the mighty King, for He has wrought salvation.

Exult, O earth, made brilliant by such splendor. Illumined by the brightness of the eternal King, know that darkness has everywhere been overcome.

Be glad, O Church our Mother, adorned with the radiance of so great a Light. Let your temple ring with the loud song of this great multitude.

And you, beloved, who are gathered near the brightness of this holy flame, invoke with me, I beg you, the mercy of almighty God:

That He who willed to number me, all unworthy, among His levites, may enlighten me with His bright light and thus enable me to sing due praises of this Christ candle.

Through the same our Lord Jesus Christ the Son who is living and reigning with God in the unity of the Holy Spirit, one God, for ever and ever.

Truly right it is and just, with all our strength of mind and heart and with our voice as instrument, to praise the invisible Father almighty, and the only-begotten Son, our Lord Jesus Christ, who paid to the eternal Father in our stead the debt of Adam, and with His own blood shed for love of us erased the ledger of ancient guilt.

For this is that Easter feast in which the true Lamb is slain, whose blood hallows the doorposts of the faithful.

This is the night in which You of old did lead our forebears, the children of Israel, out of the land of Egypt dry-shod through the Red Sea.

This is the night which scattered the darkness of sin by means of the pillar of fire.

This is the very night which delivers all who believe in Christ from worldly vice and from darkness of sin, which restores them to grace and makes them co-sharers with saints.

This is the night in which Christ burst the bonds of death and came forth as Conqueror from the grave. For unless we had been redeemed, it would avail us nothing to be born.

O wondrous condescension of Your mercy toward us!

O incomprehensible goodness of love: to redeem a slave You delivered up a Son!

O truly necessary sin of Adam, which the death of Christ has blotted out!

O happy fault, that merited so holy and so great a Redeemer!

O truly blessed night, which alone merited to know the time and hour when Christ rose from the dead!

This is the night of which it is written: "The night shall be light as the day," and: "Then shall my night be turned to day, in my rejoicing." For the holiness of this night drives out wickedness and washes away guilt; it restores innocence to the fallen and joy to the sorrowful. It banishes enmities, establishes peace, and brings low the pride of tyrants.

Wherefore, in this night of grace, receive. O holy Father, this evening sacrifice of burning light; holy Church, by the hands of her servants, offers it to You in the solemn oblation of this Candle wrought by the labor of bees. For now we have heard the praises of this column of wax which the sparkling fire lights to the honor of God. And though the fire was spread to kindle other flames, such sharing does not lessen the force of its light. For it is constantly fed by the melting wax which the mother bee wrought to form this precious Candle.

O truly blessed night, when Egypt was despoiled and Israel enriched!

O night, when heaven is wedded to earth, and God to humanity.

We ask You, therefore, Lord: may this Candle consecrated to Your honor continue with undiminished light to dispel this night's darkness. Receive it as a fragrant and pleasing offering, and let its light mingle with the lamps of heaven.

May the Morning Star behold its flame—that Morning Star who knows no setting, who rose from the pit and gently shines on all humanity.

In this festival of Easter joys, we beseech You, therefore, Lord, for ourselves Your servants, for all the clergy and Your most devoted people, for those who shepherd and guide us: grant peace to our days; guide, govern and protect us by Your constant care.

Look with favor, too, upon our rulers. Assist them with Your boundless love and gracious mercy; direct their hearts toward justice and peace, that after this life of earthly labors they may attain, together with all Your people, to the heavenly homeland.

Through the same Jesus Christ, our Lord and Your Son, who lives and reigns with You in the unity of the Holy Spirit, God, for ever and ever. Amen.

Notes

1. Adolf Adam, *The Liturgical Year: Its History and Its Meaning after the Reform of the Liturgy* (New York: Pueblo, 1981; German original, Freiburg: Herder, 1979), vii.

2. *Didachē* 14.1, in *Early Christian Fathers,* trans. C. C. Richardson (New York: Macmillan Co., 1970), 178.

3. Eusebius, *The History of the Church from Christ to Constantine,* trans. G. A. Williamson (Harmondsworth: Penguin Books, 1965), 232.

4. John Wilkinson, trans., *Egeria's Travels* (London: SPCK, 1971), 132.

5. Ibid., 253–77.

6. Ibid., 125.

7. Ibid.

8. Ibid., 86.

9. Dom Gregory Dix, *The Shape of the Liturgy* (New York: Seabury Press, 1982 [1945]), 440 n. 5.

10. John Donne, *Devotions upon Emergent Occasions,* Meditation XVII (Ann Arbor: Univ. of Michigan Press, 1959), 107–8.

11. Joseph Fitzmyer, *The Gospel according to Luke,* Anchor Bible 28, 28A (Garden City, N.Y.: Doubleday & Co., 1981, 1985), 1242.

12. *Julian of Norwich, Showings,* trans. E. Collidge and J. J. Walsh (New York: Paulist Press, 1978), 140, 144, 145, 150.

13. Ibid., 149.

14. B. F. Westcott and F. J. A. Hort, eds., *The New Testament in the Original Greek,* 2 vols. (Cambridge and London: Cambridge Univ. Press, 1881).

15. Rudolf Bultmann, *The History of the Synoptic Tradition,* trans. John Marsh, rev. ed. (New York: Harper & Row, 1963), 266* n. 1.

16. Joachim Jeremias, *The Eucharistic Words of Jesus,* rev. ed. (New York: Charles Scribner's Sons, 1966), 41–88.

17. Hugh Montefiore, *A Commentary on the Epistle to the Hebrews* (New York: Harper & Row, 1964), 181.

18. Desiderius Erasmus, *The Praise of Folly,* trans. Betty Radice (Baltimore: Penguin Books, 1971), 197–99.

19. G. K. Chesterton, "The Donkey," in *The Oxford Book of English Verse,* ed. Arthur Quiller Couch, new ed. (Oxford: Clarendon Press, 1939), 1105.

20. Rudolf Schnackenburg, *The Gospel according to John* (New York: Crossroad, 1982), 2:386.

21. Gerard, *St. Ulrich of Augsburg,* in *Patrologia Latina,* ed. J.-P. Migne (Paris, 1843–90), vol. 133, 1020ff.; see Josef Jungmann, *Pastoral Liturgy* (New York: Herder & Herder, 1962), 232; N. C. Brooks, *The Sepulchre of Christ in Art and Liturgy* (Urbana: Univ. of Illinois Press, 1921), 33–40.

22. Dix, *Shape of Liturgy,* 441.

23. John Bright, *Jeremiah,* Anchor Bible 21 (Garden City, N.Y.: Doubleday & Co., 1965), viii–ix, lviii, 267–98.

24. Ibid., 286.

25. Gerard S. Sloyan, *John,* ed. James L. Mays and Paul J. Achtemeier (Atlanta: John Knox Press, 1987), 169.

26. Schnackenburg, *Gospel according to John,* 3:20.

27. Wilkinson, *Egeria's Travels*, 137.

28. *Francis Thompson,* ed. Wilfred Meynell (Westminster, Md.: Newman Bookshop, 1947 [1913]).

29. Wilkinson, *Egeria's Travels*, 138.

30. Ibid., 276.